REVITALISING INDIAN DEMOCRACY

REVITALISING INDIAN DEMOCRACY

Major General Vinod Saighal

GYAN

Revitalising Indian Democracy

ISBN: 978-81-212-1150-5

Published in 2012 in India by
Gyan Publishing House
23, Main Ansari Road
New Delhi-110002
Phones : 23282060, 23261060
Fax : 011-23285914
E-mail: books@gyanbooks.com
Website: www.gyanbooks.com

Laser Typesetting : Quick Media, Delhi
Printed at : Chawla Offset Printers, Delhi

CONTENTS

	Preface	7
	Introduction	9
1.	**Model for Restoration of Good Government**	31
2.	**India –Vision and Reality**	39
	• Re-appraising the Idea of India	
	• Internal Threat to India's Democracy is Looming Larger with Each Passing Day	
3.	**Faltering Governance**	67
	• Turning a Blind Eye	
	• Fundamentals of Good Governance	
	• MRGG Questionnaire for Political Parties Contesting the Lok Sabha Elections	
	• Revitalising Democracy	
	• Outline of a Model President's Rule	
4.	**Elections and the Political Class**	93
	• MRGG Appeal to the Indian Voter (1996)	
	• MRGG Appeal to the Parliamentarians of the Thirteenth Lok Sabha	
	• Missive to the Court on 'Negative Vote'	
	• Indian Presidential Election 2007—A Zero Sum Game	
	• Kudos to Election Commission for Bihar Poll	
	• The Sonia Factor in Congress Victory	
	• Foreign Origin: The National Security Angle	

5. **Judiciary: The Saving Grace** 113

- Taking the PIL Route
- Need for a Collegium
- Need to Revisit Anti-Terror Laws
- Dealing with Terrorism
- Combat Scenarios
- Breaking the Definitional Impasse
- The Judicial Perspective

6. **Fountainhead of Corruption** 139

- Reconciling Coalition Dharma, Good Governance and National Security
- Court on PIL
- Skewed Debate

7. **Black Money** 159

- The New Monster

8. **Burning Issues** 167

- Regional Disparity in North East
- Social Issues—Developing Taliban-like Tendencies

9. **Jan Lok Pal Debate** 171

- Beyond the 'Jan Lok Pal Bill'
- Who Runs India ?

10. **Delhi Citizens Commission** 177

Annexures 193

Comprising petitions to the Judiciary, missives to decision makers and articles that underpin and supplement formulations in Chapters 1 to 10.

Index 257

PREFACE

Unveiling the Model for Restoration of Good Government (MRGG) ten months after retirement at the India International Centre, New Delhi in October 2005, I stumbled into the domain of good governance purely by accident. It was an intellectual exercise and nothing more.

Working on aspects related to global governance that were to form part of my book *Third Millennium Equipoise* (it came out later in 1998), I decided to extrapolate a few ideas for the presentation at the IIC. The Director, India International Centre at the time (now governor J&K) who had chaired the session was kind enough to circulate copies of the paper that I had left with him after the talk. Over the following months, surprise of surprises, several features of the model were adopted, in principle, by many NGOs in the country working in this field. It got translated into Spanish and French and several Indian languages. Meanwhile, the UN Secretary General had it circulated in the UN and the President of the European Commission who was from Luxembourg (I had been additionally accredited to that country in the second half of the 1980s) got the Model circulated in Brussels. Somewhere along the way, by mid-1996, the Model had become a Movement, retaining the same acronym. Hereafter, MRGG stood for Movement for Restoration of Good Government instead of Model for Restoration of Good Government. I was co-opted as its Convener.

Not long after, realization dawned that I had put my foot into it. All attempts to extricate myself in order to concentrate on other areas of interest proved futile. After 16 years of what started as an intellectual exercise, not only have I not been able to pull my foot out, I find that I am into it with both feet.

The MRGG is a universal model that with modification can be up-scaled to work at the global level or in any country in the world. Conversely, it can be scaled down and applied at the state, city or local levels. Following from the first effort there are other formulations in the book that have attracted considerable interest in the country and abroad. The reader is invited to share my humble travails added to countless others working towards it to put India on a sounder democratic footing.

Vinod Saighal

INTRODUCTION

An exercise carried out to scan old copies of the newspapers of leading dailies in 1993,1994,1995 revealed that the terms 'good governance' or 'good government' were not in vogue. In fact, these were hardly ever raised. Except for an odd flurry when a former army chief reportedly stated that good governance was very much their business, the newspapers and the electronic media were mostly busy fighting corruption, horse-trading and bribing for votes.

It is only after 1996 that the term 'good government' gained currency. It is not inconceivable that the Model as well as the Movement for Restoration of Good Government (MRGG) had a role to play in the adoption of these terms. The early years after the inception of the movement were spent in creating voter awareness, awareness amongst parliamentarians (a nearly impossible task) and presentation of follow up papers on the subject of good governance.

The voter awareness appeal sent out by MRGG found resonance in many parts of the country. Coming into the new century MRGG, having gained in confidence was able to contribute far more in what had become a national endeavor to make government more transparent and responsive to the needs of the people.

Having by now established its presence in the good governance domain and having won a fair measure of respect from different strata of society the convener felt bold enough to take part in PILs before the Supreme Court (for example MRGG was a signatory for the famous affidavits case that obliges individuals standing for elections to provide details of their background).

Furthermore, several petitions on some of the burning issues of the day were sent to the chief justices of the Supreme Court. Although justices of the higher judiciary do not respond in writing to letters received, in a few cases the judgments delivered did give an indication that the public petitions had not been ignored. By about the middle of the first decade of the new century papers presented by MRGG at national and occasionally in international fora were treated with respect. A very limited overview of some areas where MRGG has made a contribution in the field of good government follows in the ensuing paragraphs. Readers going through the book are likely to be rewarded by richer fare.

Decriminalising the Polity: A Ray of Hope

In the two talks delivered at the India International Centre on the subject of rising criminalisation of the polity and allied aspects the difficulty of arresting the trend had been touched upon. It is a given that the political parties will be reluctant to amend the Representation of People Act 1951 to exclude "serious" criminals from standing for elections, "winnability" at all costs being one of the overriding criteria for allocating seats. In the case of the judiciary a Chief Justice in his pronouncements had held out scant hope for the Supreme Court intervening. That leaves the Election Commission itself. The Election Commission has to take up the slack to prevent the government from becoming a government 'of the criminals for the criminals'. It is well known that in the state assemblies and at the Centre several cases of "serious" criminals with charge sheets against them for heinous crimes have become ministers.

The Constitution has very clearly made the Election Commission responsible for "holding free and fair elections". This is the operative, unfettered clause that gives the Election Commission the overarching responsibility for ensuring that elections are "free and fair", to the extent that money and muscle power are excluded, thus saving the voter from intimidation or coercion. Flowing from this the Election Commission would be well within its rights to mandate that 'enough is enough'; and that it would henceforth reject the candidature of serious criminals from standing for elections. This *suo motu* action by the Election Commission would enjoy the whole-hearted support of citizens of the country across the board, or at least the overwhelming majority of them. Some political parties might fall in line. However, the possibility exists that other parties with large number of legislators with criminal backgrounds might go to the Supreme Court against the Election Commission's decision. In such a case it would be well on the cards that a Constitution Bench of the Supreme Court would uphold the decision of the Election Commission.

In seminars held on the subject since this proposition was first articulated, several legal luminaries, including a former Chief Justice of the SC had opined that the suggestion had considerable merit. At a discussion held on 'paid news' by the Centre for Media Studies on May 10, 2010 at the India International Centre, where the then Chief Election Commissioner was present, the Chairman, former Cabinet Secretary Shri B.G. Deshmukh in his concluding remarks had opined that the Election Commission *did* have the scope for a more 'liberal' interpretation of its constitutional mandate to hold 'free and fair elections'.

Evidently, should the Election Commission decide to act on the suggestion made above, along with the announcement of the date of the elections, it would have to announce to all concerned that it would reject the applications of known "serious" criminals (the term has been amplified in the relevant chapter) from standing for election. Civil society organisations have to come together to press home this point with the Election Commission to check the descent into terminal degeneracy. Commenting upon civil society's continuing plethora of seminars, articles and emails complaining of government inaction on this long overdue reform, one journalist summed up their effort beautifully with a pithy line in Urdu: "*Kaun sunta hai tooti ki niqarkhane mein*", (who listens to a poor (she) parrot in a place where huge drums are being sounded)"? In the same vein another observer of the scene wrote: "*idhar udhar ki baat mat kar, yeh to bata kafila kis ne loota* ?" And finally a comment from a NNFI (National Network for India) source, "Mother India has no mama, papa".

An enormous amount of construction activity has been taking place in Delhi. The activity, if anything, is likely to pick up in the coming years. While major projects would be - or should be - receiving attention from professional monitoring agencies, it is the lesser activity that does not get the critical scrutiny that it deserves. A case in point is the ripping up and resetting of pavements that has been going on non-stop for several years, irrespective of whether the existing pavements were in good shape or not. Whatever the reason for the pavement replacement exercise at heavy cost the fact remains that the new flagstone paving is not uniformly good. At some places, closer to VIP areas the quality appears to be good. This is certainly not the case in many other areas where the pavements are giving way or deteriorating within weeks and months of completion of the work. In several places it is unacceptably sub-standard. In the earlier years once the pavements were laid they remained well-embedded, firm and in good condition for years and even decades on end. The present replacement drive simply does not measure up to the earlier standards. Maintenance and repair are required within the first year, if not earlier.

In the light of the foregoing, it would be appropriate for an independent monitoring cell to be set up by the Lt. Governor. It would be tasked to prepare a report on the quality of the work undertaken in this regard since the pavement replacement scheme was created to review: the cost of material, embedding and laying techniques, material used, quality of fill and compacting before the placing of paving, quality of finish, cost of construction as well as the contractual obligations for quality of work, durability, penalty clauses for poor work and the like. Similar exercise to be undertaken for disposal of malba, cost of paving stones recovered from the replaced pavements (the majority of these being in good condition), recycling, if any, and the timeliness of repair when cracks appear (and before these get enlarged and start ruining larger portions of the pavement). The quality of periodic monitoring by the officials of the concerned departments farming out the contracts and for maintaining the pavements in good condition at all times is of the utmost importance. Several other details need to be gone into. Unless strict vigil is maintained by all concerned during construction the quality of the work invariably suffers. In all cases where the monitoring agency or cell finds that shortcuts have been taken strict action should be taken against the defaulters. Their names and the action taken against them must be put on departmental websites for public scrutiny.

The most important threats for humanity and all life forms on the planet are undoubtedly global warming and climate change. There are hardly any international bodies, countries or NGOs in this domain that are not seized of it. The number of international, regional and local meetings that take place on the issue are legion. One of the most urgent problems remains the increasing levels of CO_2 in the atmosphere. Many mitigation techniques from carbon sequestration to carbon credits among others are being considered to reduce carbon levels. That being the case it must be one of the most amazing conundrums that one of the simplest pathways to ameliorate the situation at little or no cost is ignored by world bodies and governments and by the numerous conferences taking place on the subject around the world.

Simply stated, it is the heedless method of exploitation of natural resources and the accompanying displacement of local communities that invariably takes place, mainly in the developing world and the pristine forest regions (where local communities have been living as pastoral societies engaged in gathering forest produce, using methods that they have practiced for centuries), leading to shrinking habitats still rich in biodiversity. Most of these communities are to be found in developing countries in Africa, Latin America and Southeast and South Asia. They are that part of humanity whose carbon footprint even in the 21st century is extremely low, some time almost non-existent. This realization has either not dawned on decision-makers or governments and vested interests simply turn a blind eye to it. Numerous examples can be given from around the world. A few of them fresh in the public mind will suffice.

In Myanmar, the new government has decided to stop the construction of a mega-dam being built by China on the Myitsone River in upper Myanmar. The Chinese government having already sunk in a fair amount of money into the preliminary works is furious. It is to be hoped that the Government of Myanmar will stick to its decision and what is more halt the planned construction of mega-dams elsewhere on the Myitsone and Irrawady rivers. Had the construction not been stopped what would have been the outcome. The Myanmar government would have earned money from electricity, 90 percent of which would have been sold to China. The hidden costs of these gargantuan projects hardly get publicized. It has been estimated that approximately one hundred thousand people would have been displaced. These people have already suffered due to clear felling of a sizeable forest area, as has been the case for the mega-dams built earlier. Some of the displaced forest dwellers and pastoral societies living in the area might have found work as laborers under Chinese construction bosses. The large majority would have been sent to other sites and put in shanty towns for perpetual ghetto-ised existence.

The second example is from the tribal societies known as 'adivasis' in the eastern state of Odisha in India. Large-scale mining activities have taken place or are in the pipeline in areas where the adivasis live as they have lived undisturbed for hundreds, if not thousands of years. Mining is also planned by mining leviathans in a pristine tract called the Nyamgiri Hills sacred to the adivasis from time immemorial. The damage already done by the bauxite mines has resulted in heavy pollution of the area: disease inducing toxins in the water bodies, where even the animals (although seldom recorded) that come to drink suffer as much as the humans. Protestors are routinely beaten up by the police and several killed. Compensation is offered. It has been mostly rejected by the adivasis who would not like their centuries-old traditions that hardly leave *any* carbon footprint to be disturbed. Selected leaders of the protest movements are likely to be made to fall in line by hefty bribes - standing operating procedure worldwide. Even the compensation to the adivasis will be increased. Again at what cost to the environment and the natural guardians of the environment, the forest dwellers whose lands are expropriated. Only two examples have been given. They are representative of the tribulations of the indigenous communities displaced by governments allied to global mining lobbies bent upon destroying pristine tracts around the world; where so-called modernization is being forced upon hapless people who have been the guardians of the undisturbed forest habitats so critical for habitability of the planet for future generations of humans and the flora and fauna that has managed to survive.

A word on the fate that awaits displaced communities forcibly removed from their land and way of life. They are resettled in ghetto-like shanty towns or even concrete blocks. Either way the disoriented elders spend their time bemoaning their loss while the youngsters drift into drugs, drunkenness, prostitution and the other ills of modernity into which they have been forced. Lacking survival skills for the new life that they are required to lead many of them drift into cities into a life of crime or destitution in the hovels known as 'bastis' (in India) and 'favellas' (in Latin America) where they end up. The lands that they have left behind are ravaged. Animal and bird life soon disappears due to the extreme pollution of the water bodies and the toxins that leach into the soil. Even in their marginalized condition their carbon footprint automatically rises in the city.

Unsustainable economic development has not been reined in, despite all the climate change conferences.

Capitalism capitalises on human greed. That's why it is called capitalism. China and India will not forgo development, as they still have a long way to go before ameliorating poverty, leave alone eradicating it. The economic bottom-line of the largely unfettered corporate world must include an environmental bottom-line that will translate into ecological sustainability, if the planet is to survive. In his concluding remarks from a presentation at Basel before the 19th IPPNW Conference, (International Physicians for the Prevention of Nuclear War) in August 2010 the author stated: "The large economies pushing toward very high growth do *not* seem to be concerned about future generations. The tragedy is compounded by the rest of the world that is undergoing recession pangs pushing for greater consumption by China and India. In short, nobody seems to be concerned about the future of our children or the coming generations. We are heading toward planetary destruction here and now. China and India still want GDP increase in double digits when most of this growth is predicated on higher energy consumption levels based largely on abundant coal reserves, the burning of which is most conducive for global warming and climate change. In fact, the consequences of double digit or very high GDP growth in the case of countries with large populations are such that this high digit growth can be termed as obscene. China, overtaking the world's largest car producer, saw its passenger car vehicle sales zoom 47.5 percent, from 5.7 million units in 2008 to 8.4 million units in 2009, *in just one year*. India registered 24.5 percent jump in passenger car vehicle sales from 1.5 million units in 2009 to about 1.9 million units in 2010 in the domestic market. Should this trend, egged on by the rest of the world for greater consumption to underpin the global economy continue for just 10 more years these two countries, without even counting USA, Brazil, South Africa and Nigeria would be able to incinerate the planet by their scorching pace of growth, with attendant environmental destruction on a scale not witnessed earlier on the planet, well before the next nuclear related mishap. It is time to take stock. Time is not running out for critical decisions that should have been in place by now; it has already run out. The human race is now running on borrowed time". Unquote.

A story going around on the internet goes as follows:

Once upon a time a king and all his family died, so a well- to-do man was invited to be "king", by "popular" support. The new "king" gave in to every request for money from the treasury. He said "yes" to all schemes and made merry himself.

One day when it was all coming to a close, and balances became near non-existent, his supporters asked him "What now?"

The "king" picked up his stick and said, "I've done my bit as expected and now I shall walk away".

This is exactly what is happening in the states as well as at the Centre. Deplete the exchequer by populist schemes; make your billions unhindered knowing that in the present dispensation prosecution becomes extremely difficult and time consuming and walk away to wallow in wealth for several generations, for that is the scale of the loot and damage to the economy.

The decline in governance at the Centre has reached proportions that in many parts of the country mere mention of Delhi often conjures up visions of shameless corruption at the apex of governance, in whose hands the destiny of India has been reposed by the electorate. In spite of all the scams that have brought down the image of the Indian government in the world as well as the PILs before the courts, the real depth of the terminal degradation has still not been fully appreciated. The Anna Hazare movement has certainly stirred the conscience of citizens where ever they happen to be. Innocently they have put their hopes in the Lokpal Bill, which even if enacted to the satisfaction of all those who have backed it, the improvement in governance or the elimination of corruption at the highest levels is not likely to be achieved any time soon. As the saying goes 'there is many a slip between the cup and the lip'. Relating to the deviousness of those who run the government, the aphorism can be taken one step further, 'there can be one more slip between the lip and the lip'.

The reason is simple. Should a formidable Lokpal body really get going the majority of the lot at the very apex of government, would either land up in jail or have to flee the country. Therefore, even should a satisfactory enactment take place the government can, if past experience is a guide: delay, divert attention, bring in extraneous issues, not frame the rules in time, delay notification and so many other ploys that have been refined by the dynasty and their coterie that has held on to power for such a long time. What people do not seem to realise is that there are many ways in which governance has been subverted and corruption institutionalized that will always remain beyond the remit of even the most determined Lokpal bodies. A few examples will suffice.

Whenever heads of government bodies, institutions or PSUs retire or demit office their replacement is interminably delayed by line ministries, appointment committees, PMO or on orders from 'above'. The explanation is fairly obvious. When positions are left vacant there is no outside mechanism that can prevent all those who are able to, from taking full advantage of the vacuum created, during the period that there is no functional, duly appointed head. At times the number two in the headless body, otherwise fit for occupying the top slot is kept on tenterhooks till approval is forthcoming. During the interim he or she would be in no position to resist the demands emanating from the line ministries and bureaucrats, including personal assistants, lower-level functionaries and others. In short, this is the period when any and everyone who is in a position to do so take full advantage of the situation.

That is not all. More often than not the top position is kept vacant so that bureaucrats can hold the fort. This has the dual advantage of allowing the civil servant officiating to take all the perks that would be available to the head of the organization as well as continue to avail facilities enjoyed as a senior official in the ministry. Thus the person or the ministry that is required to sit in judgment or exercise supervision ends up by sitting on judgment on itself, i.e., zero accountability and full freedom to bilk the institution and appoint relations, friends or others on requests received from above or at intermediate and lower levels. What is more the Joint Secretary having dual charge is unable to do justice to the institution that he/she temporarily heads. The number of good institutions or PSUs that have been ruined by such practices is too large to list individually. Air India is a good example. How many bureaucrats rather than the best of professionals have been selected by independent committees to head the once world renowned airline, now brought to its knees after having drained the exchequer of subsidies and enriched ministers heading the civil aviation portfolio. Besides the public does any one in the government really care? Seeing what happens at the Centre the States not only follow suit, they go one step better.

In a perceptive article in the editorial of *The Statesman* (New Delhi Friday 25 November, 2011) a well known journalist had this to say on the state of governance in the country. "Today we have police stations without having the rule of law. We have law courts without getting justice. We have elections without having democracy. Our system has collapsed because our democratic institutions have been destroyed. Institutions have been reduced to empty husks devoid of real contents". In this regard an excerpt from *The Tribune* dated November 1, 2011 under the heading 'Tainted cops retained in service, High Court seeks details from DGP' is reproduced below: "The Punjab and Haryana High Court wants to know from the Haryana Director-General of Police the details of police officials retained in service after having faced department proceedings in cases of moral turpitude and acceptance of illegal gratification.........................

Less than a fortnight ago, the Bench of acting Chief Justice MM Kumar and Justice Rajiv Narain Raina had also stayed the operation of a circular issued by the Punjab Director-General of Police on May 18, 2010. The DGP, vide the circular, had directed all appointing authorities in the Police Department not to remove a police official convicted for a criminal offence for which the sentence prescribed under the IPC is less than three years. The DGP had also recommended leniency against them".

The first question that arises on reading the news item is "Why are the police heads issuing such outrageous instructions". For the general public the immediate answer that would come to mind could very well be "because so many of them are in the same boat". Although accurate statistics would be difficult to come by, the public perception might not be that far off the mark. This is just one of the instances where the High Court has acted on a petition filed before it.

In actual fact it is the operative norm for the police in practically every state. It is not only the DGPs of Haryana and Punjab in the present case, even the political masters are inclined to condone actions of this nature because quite a few of the criminal episodes are the result of unrecorded instructions given by them to senior police officers as well as directly to those lower down the chain. Some high-minded, professional police heads have tried to break this nexus, to no effect. It could have also been one of the reasons for the PIL filed in the Supreme Court by a former DGP, Shri Prakash Singh. Following the PIL the Supreme Court gave directions in 2006 for the Centre and the states to revisit the 1861 Police Act and bring it in line with the recommendations of the Police Commissions as modified and updated in subsequent reviews*. To date neither the centre nor the states have complied with the Supreme Court directive in letter *and* spirit.

At a talk delivered on countering terrorism to a cross section of police and paramilitary officers some time ago, one of the police officers put the speaker wise by offering his view that in his state at least, if not other states as well, it was incorrect to assume that MLAs were hankering only after mantri's chair. A large number of them preferred to exercise control over the SHO and police thanas in their constituencies. It allowed them to have false cases registered against opponents and prevent the filing of FIRs against their kith and kin. This is exactly what notorious bahubalis have been doing in many states since long.

Reverting to the news item cited above, the public has to be made aware that the practice described in Haryana and Punjab might well be the standard operating procedure throughout the country. On a number of occasions, statements issued by the police appear in the press that the policeman (or policemen) charged with grave misconduct or crime has been suspended or sent to police lines. The public seldom, if ever, gets to know the final disposition of the case. Unless the media remains alert in the more serious cases or the judiciary takes cognizance the chances are that the suspended police person sent to police lines would be reassigned once the furore dies down, or the investigation of the case delayed indefinitely. While individuals can file the occasional RTI*, it is only sustained investigative journalism

---

*The need for police reforms in India is long recognised. It has been almost three decades of discussion by government created committees and commissions. Way back in 1979 the National Police Commission (NPC) was set up to report on policing and give recommendations for reform. The Commission produced eight reports, dozens of topic specific recommendations and also a Model Police Act.

None of the major recommendations were adopted by any government. This persuaded two former Director Generals of Police (DGPs) in 1996 to file a public interest litigation (PIL) in the Supreme Court asking the court to direct governments to implement the NPC recommendations. In the course of the 10 year long case, in 1998 the court set up the Ribeiro Committee which handed in its reports in 1999. This was followed by the Padmanabhaiah Committee report in 2000 and eventually the Police Act Drafting Committee (PADC or Soli Sorabjee Committee) that drafted a new model police bill to replace the colonial 1861 Police Act. Meanwhile precious little was done on

or an omnibus directive by the higher judiciary that can ensure that action taken in all such cases is made available for scrutiny by the courts at laid down periodicities and the information displayed on websites in each police district.

Continuing saga of security lapses, the government has been expending enormous energy, time and effort of the agencies that it controls to muddy and close the Bofors case, let Mr. Q off the hook, target opponents and whitewash black money trails abroad, on orders from above. Had even a portion of this effort been expended to safeguard the security of India and its people, instead of foreign interests, the country would not have been exposed to terror attacks at such frequency, with relative ease. The police forces are demoralised, badly equipped, lack training and good leadership. Despite the promises made post-Mumbai, proper coordination of intelligence through a unified and autonomous agency remains a wish list. Internal and external security remain severely compromised due to lack of political will to act. The political class needs to urgently come together on this subject and act in the interest of the nation. What they need to do has been repeated all too often. The country desperately needs more governance and less of political interference.

Born to Rule was the title of a book that came out a long time ago. Applied to democracy in India in the 21st century

---

the ground to improve policing or implement recommendations put forth by any of these committees or commissions. It was only a decade later in 2006 that the Court delivered its verdict. In what is popularly referred to as the Prakash Singh case the Supreme Court ordered that reform must take place. The states and union territories were directed to comply with seven binding directives that would kick start reform. These directives pulled together the various strands of improvement generated since 1979. The Court required immediate implementation of its orders either through executive orders or new police legislation. At first the Court itself monitored compliance of all States and Union Territories. However in 2008 the Court decided to set up a three member Monitoring Committee with a two year mandate to examine compliance state by state and report back to it periodically.

and the dynasties that have come to the fore at the Centre and some of the States, 'Born to Misrule' would be the better appellation. Leaders in India always seem to wax eloquent on India's 'Unity in Diversity'. So much is the emphasis placed on this unity that it has become part of the national lore of the country, in India and abroad. Looked at closely, however, the hollowness of this high sounding claim reveals itself. There might still have been a semblance of unity in diversity for a few decades after independence with people's minds fresh about the horrors visited upon the subcontinent, when the country was partitioned almost overnight along the line demarcated by the infamous Radcliffe Award. Lately the political leaders have seen to it that whatever unity was forged during the early period is sundered by them in every way possible: vote bank politics; perpetuation and expansion of reservation; dynastic politics leading to lack of inner party democracy; looting of the exchequer; crony capitalism; allowing foreign interests to influence decisions (Quatrochi was not the only case); criminalizing of the polity; pogroms - the main ones being the killing of Sikhs orchestrated by the Congress in 1984 and the killing of Muslims in Gujarat under a BJP chief minister. The list is endless. Where then is the much vaunted unity that leaders keep mouthing from every pulpit?

Coming to think of it, the only unity in diversity today is that of over-arching criminality, self-aggrandizement and the promotion of dynastic or party interest at the cost of national interest. As it happens, a former governor of the Reserve Bank of India has gone on record to say that he found that often decisions taken by the leaders furthered their own or the party's interest at the cost of the national interest. One just has to pause and carry out a survey across the country to see how a negative unity in diversity has been institutionalized. Although examples are plentiful, a few illustrations will suffice. When the British transferred power to the natives (about whom they always had misgivings as to their ability to govern) every hill station in the country was a jewel to behold. Today there is hardly any hill station that has not been reduced to a sorry state: Darjeeling, Kalimpong, Gangtok, Shimla, Nainital and so many others that present a shocking contrast to anybody who had seen them earlier. Talking of corruption and mal-governance or absence of effective government there is a strong unity between the Centre and the States, with the odd exception bucking the trend from time to time, Bihar under Nitish Kumar being a case in point. Take another example that of municipalities or municipal corporations. There is an elected representatives' guild that ensures that of the thousands of municipalities hardly any one of them is free from corruption, misrule or urban neglect: be it hygiene, sewage systems, health, water and electricity supply, waste disposal or retaining the aesthetic harmony of the once beautiful Indian cities. The list is endless. It includes: pollution of rivers including the sacred Ganga and Jamuna, disappearing water bodies, encroachment into forests, decline in wetlands, flora and fauna, including the decline in the number of the animal that is the pride of India, the Tiger.

Based on the negative list enumerated above, to borrow a term from trade negotiation between countries, there can hardly be any doubt that the only unity that prevails today is the negative unity in diversity or disunity in diversity. Until there is a sea change in ethics, morality, the quality of leaders, and the way in which the country is governed, elected leaders should refrain from telling a pack of lies to the nation and the world of the positive unity in diversity, which is a figment of their imagination. Under the leadership of netas across the political spectrum any claim to unity remains a patent falsehood.

The titular Head of the State is the Office of the President of India. An office envisaged by our Founding Fathers as being occupied by persons of high probity, wisdom and a deep sense of the responsibility of the Chair. Over time Corruption, in the broadest sense of the term, has entered what should be a hallowed domain: it is now very often occupied by those of dubious reputation; of highly political backgrounds and affiliation; of individuals indebted to political authorities, thus resulting in their inability to take considered and independent decisions with the National Interest being paramount. Instead they tend to carry out orders with distinctly biased intentions. Surely now is the time to revisit the criteria laid down by our own leaders at the start of the journey to make India a land of the just and the free.

Over a year after the much talked about Commonwealth Games, New Delhi in October 2010, the manner of build up to the games, the enormous corruption and the poor quality of construction still continue to cause ripples; The main reason being that the very top echelons seem to have totally gotten away with it, without even a passing mention to criminal cases being filed against them. At some future date with the change of government should the cases against the highest level culprits ever be reopened, it will be found that all proof of their complicity would have been obliterated. This has been the case for some of the lower ranking people against whom charges have been filed as well.

What the people of India and the world at large find inexplicable is the total passivity of practically every higher up living in Delhi who could have intervened but chose to remain silent; as if they were being driven around the capital city blindfolded. For what else explains the apathy, indifference or studied silence of the President of India, Vice President and so many others who had nothing to do with the awarding of contracts or overseeing the build up. Then there was the entire governance chain from top to bottom at the centre, starting with chairperson of the UPA and Lt Governor and the Chief Minister of Delhi. While the public, the media and even the foreign press and visiting dignitaries left no doubt about their misgivings to what was happening, no responsible person in the government intervened except at the last minute in order to ensure that the ultimate shame is not brought upon the country should the facilities not be ready. As it turns out, they were finally made ready just as the first contingent of foreign participants was touching down at Delhi airport.

The government might comprise the UPA, the build up to the Commonwealth Games and the handling or more appropriately the misappropriation of public monies was entirely a Congress Party show, some say being micro-managed as usual at the highest levels by the sons and the sons-in-law of those at the apex. Needless to say the truth will never come out. All tracks whether in Delhi, Switzerland or elsewhere would have been covered and any trace of them obliterated. There are those who say that the DTAT with Switzerland was signed to ensure that all cases prior to the Treaty's coming into force on 1st January 2012 would be whitewashed as the treaty would be operative prospectively after that date. In this regard excerpt from *The Statesman* (New Delhi 25 September 2011) is reproduced: "The Swiss Ambassador to India has indicated that the Double Taxation Agreement with his country would be applicable with effect from 1 January 2012, prospective applicability, or make retrospective applicability far more difficult, which in turn means that those who now have black money stashed away in Swiss banks could get away Scot free". Unquote

That governance is in terminal decline becomes clear from the CAG Report on the Commonwealth Games. As in the case of the most sophisticated money-launderers and their cross holdings in companies that would make it very difficult or impossible to catch them out, the crisscrossing pattern of responsibilities that presaged the Games revealed a much higher degree of sophistication to prevent detection post facto. Under the heading ***Who called the shots? It was a bhool bhulaiya of committees*** the Report goes on to say: "Nowhere is the tangled web of deceit in which the CWG was trapped more starkly visible than in the structure set up to organize it. The CAG has a double spread, color-coded organogram showing the tangled web in all its glory. There were at least 31 decision making bodies, 22 advisory bodies and 16 implementing agencies, apart from 34 'functional area', another name for 'work to be done'. You can imagine the number of crisscrossing lines that connect all these to each other. It is a *bhool bhulaiya,* with committees, sub-committees and groups that are created and disbanded for over five years, even as 10 central ministries, the PMO, central bureaucracy engaged with the Delhi government, its Lt-Governor. On top of this, there is an OC with its committees, officers and fast track panels. The PMO set up a core group of ministers, an interim group of ministers, a new group of ministers, an apex committee (with five sub-groups)– even as the cabinet set up a committee of secretaries, a finance sub committee, an empowered finance sub-committee. This is just the central government's top echelons getting a piece of action. Imagine what is going on under each of the 10 ministries. Concerning sports venues, basically stadiums the CWG venues were 'owned' by 15 different bodies. Their development was under a stadium committee, itself under a venue coordination committee, overseen by an Infrastructure Monitoring Committee, supervised by a general Coordination Committee and also an Infrastructure Coordination Committee, all under the sports ministry. The venue owners were themselves under seven different ministries apart from the LG and the NDMC. Besides, the COO and the CEO of the OC chaired by Suresh Kalmadi were also 'looking after' the venues, including purchases. Meanwhile the PWD was under the Delhi government.....you get the idea". To encapsulate, there were 10 central ministers involved, 31 Decision-making bodies, 22 advisory bodies, 16 Implementing agencies, 23 Sub Committees, 5 Sub groups. *(Times News Network, The Times of India,* New Delhi Saturday August 16, 2011 P # 6).

Forget the opposition and their criticism of the government. It follows a pattern of opposing everything the government does whether good for the country or bad. What about all the Congress ministers and members of parliament who live in bungalows and houses in New Delhi. Why did they shut their eyes to what was happening? Not one of them opened their mouth. They might not have been privy to everything that was going on practically everyday. Surely they knew that all was not well whenever they stepped out of their houses, sometimes several times a day. The people of India would be forgiven for thinking that their loyalty is only to the person who makes them ministers or Prime Minister or at whose behest tickets are allotted. The loyalty to that person evidently overrides the loyalty to their country. Not one of them got up to expose what was happening.

At the height of the criticism of the poor quality of work and late start for the build up to the Commonwealth Games that was being reflected in the foreign press a former Ambassador wrote: 'I have been Ambassador to China for many years and then for an equal number of years to India. I was very impressed with China's growth. During my tenure in India I found that India has some of the finest professionals in the world. When they leave India they are snapped up by the largest multinationals from many countries. Why is it that when so much was at stake for India's reputation the government never entrusted the professionals available in the country to oversee their most prestigious programmes'. After the missive from the Ambassador there is nothing left to say, because it was a systematic, orchestrated loot the parallels to which would be difficult to find even in the most discredited African dictatorships where the likes of Mobuto are said to have driven their countries to the bottom of the heap.

From past experience it would seem that even the special SIT set up by the Supreme Court in the illegal foreign money case might not be able to get to the bottom of it. It is because the investigative agencies over the last few years have been thoroughly subverted to safeguard the interest of those at the apex of governance, more so the extra-constitutional authority that has been wielding near absolute power in

India without any accountability whatsoever, either to the parliament, the executive or the people of India. It is a perfectly Machiavellian ploy of governance through remote control that has destroyed the parliamentary democracy system of the Prime Minister and his council of ministers. If continued any longer, it will further degrade the process of governance and accountability and end up by completely undermining democratic functioning and the constitution. In fact, the time may have come for a special SIT nominated by the Supreme Court to examine the functioning of the extra-judicial entity as well as the coterie surrounding it, which, for all practical purposes has been operating above the law and whose corruption-related activities as reported in the press seem to be immune from any investigation. That foreign interests may on occasion be influencing the decisions of the remote controllers of government cannot be discounted.

Two decades have passed since the Vohra Committee Report on the nexus between politicians-civil servants and criminals. Not only has there been no progress in breaking the nexus, the report, like many other important reports (for example, the Henderson Brooks Commission report on the 1962 China War debacle) has not been available in the public domain. If anything, the nexus has deepened and expanded to include foreign interests and is now threatening the vitals of Indian democracy and the security of the Republic. Does anyone seriously believe that the present dispensation that runs the country and has taken the rot much, much further is in a position to stem the rot. So, short of a revolution, who is going to deflect this body blow being delivered to democracy and the Constitution? Only the Supreme Court has the ability to set things right this side of anarchy in the country.

Similar chaos obtains in most other areas of governance as became evident on 26/11, 13/7 and now the case of the large ship floating into harbour undetected by the navy, the coast guard, Mumbai Police, and all central government and Maharashtra government agencies involved in safeguarding

India's security. Is it any wonder that the citizens of the country and well-wishers of India are seriously questioning whether the government of India at the apex, as presently constituted, has the ability to safeguard national security? In fact, such is the colossal lack of competence displayed that many people have started wondering whether the glaring loopholes in India's security are being deliberately overlooked or not addressed with the urgency that they deserve. The situation is best described by another writer. Filip Tunjic writing in *"The Journal of Slavic Military Studies"* (Vol. 12, No. 2, June 1999) states: "At the same time, instead of a state 'drowning' in the globalization processes and instead of the state functions of governing being reduced, an inversive is taking place - an intensive alienation of a state from its own constitutional base that is its own people, when the governing political elites, often strongly connected with criminal groups and corrupt officials, are governing the state and need people less and less". What Filip Tunjic says is unexceptionable. If not already the case, it is becoming increasingly applicable to India due to the downward spiral in public life. And this brings us to the most important question before us today: "How will the downward spiral be reversed? Who will reverse it?" Over to the reader.

1

MODEL FOR RESTORATION OF GOOD GOVERNMENT

Introduction

The Model for Restoration of Good Government (MRGG) is a universal model which in its local derivative in each country becomes the Movement for Restoration of Good Government (the same acronym). MRGG differs from all other political parties. In that, capturing political power per se (to form a government) is not its objective. The Movement aims at establishing a presence in the political mainstream to the extent that it can exercise a benign over-watch. It will ensure that its tenets, which are essentially those enshrined in the Constitution of the country, are not flouted with impunity by politicians in power. With this in mind, the founders of the Movement would have to abide by a blueprint whereby its adherents will eschew political office; and to ensure that they do not ultimately go the way of all flesh and assume the role of king makers for years on end (by their continued presence in the highest decision-making body of the MRGG) they will completely remove themselves from the political scene every five years. Similarly, in a major conceptual departure from the manner in which political parties function the world over, the MRGG will not enrol party members on a permanent basis. It will instead provide a forum for like-minded people, coming together for varying periods of time, for the sole purpose of ensuring that a check is maintained on elected representatives of the people; and that the national interest is not sacrificed for personal or party ends.

The model being presented has an universal applicability. It is amenable to (sensible) modifications to suit local conditions. The guiding principles which govern the model can be stated briefly. These are:

- The change has to be effected through the ballot box. There need not be a witch hunt. Tainted leaders who wish to fade away gracefully should be allowed to do so.
- Restoration of institutional vigour in the bodies that constitute the government is the best guarantee against misuse of power.
- The new force emerging for the restoration of good government should not itself become degenerate over a period of time. Hence, the Trustees of the process of restoration must remain faceless - shunning public office and publicity. By the same token, people who show signs of personal ambition must be allowed to go their own way no matter how worthy their contribution is in exposing the bad ways of the present incumbents.

Aims and Objects

The MRGG aims to restore dignity, decency and decorum to the body politic.

It aims to restore the primacy of the rule of law and to revitalise good governance in the country adopting the model by :—

(a) Promoting effective governance at all levels by excluding political interference in the day-to-day work of the civil services and law and order forces.

(b) Upholding the principal of accountability al all levels of governance.

(c) Support of public action litigation by concerned citizens' action groups.

(d) Supporting special legislation for the removal and prosecution of corrupt ministers (the Italian and

French models of independent prosecutors could be adopted with suitable modifications).

(e) Strengthening the agencies for effective monitoring and protection of the environment.

(f) Eschewing caste-based politics and communalism in any form and by upholding the spirit of the Constitution.

The MRGG will invite like-minded people to participate in its struggle to restore dignity and decorum to the process of governance. (In India the Mahatma has shown the way to India and the world in the earlier decades of this century. Wherever democratic norms are being eroded, the people at the grassroots are ready to carry forward the struggle in the closing decade of the Century).

Charter

The core of the MRGG comprises a Governing Council and its Secretary General. The Convenor (founder) of the Movement will be its (ex-officio) Secretary General. His first order of business will be to set up a framework for the functioning of the MRGG in consonance with its Charter. At the national level, the policies of the MRGG will be laid down by the Governing Council comprising eleven members. The first Governing Council will be selected from a panel of fifty names put before the Eminent Hundred by the Convenor of the MRGG. The Eminent Hundred would be nationally respected figures, who by their pre-eminence in their respective fields and selfless conduct have won the respect of the nation, cutting across party affiliations and all other barriers of race, cast, creed or sex. The Eminent Hundred come into play in the model just once for selecting the first Governing Council. Thereafter, they have no further role to play as the process becomes self-sustaining and self-cleansing. Essentially there would not be much difference in the criteria for preparing the panel of fifty names which would be circulated by the Convenor (first Secretary General of the MRGG) to the Eminent Hundred for giving their preference of eleven members for the first Governing Council of the MRGG. The background, eminence and credibility of persons figuring in the panel for the Governing Council (members) would essentially be the same as for the Eminent Hundred. The Eminent Hundred do not have to come together to sit in a conclave. The panel from which the Governing Council is to be selected would be circulated to them individually for indicating their preference. They would be at liberty to reject the entire panel and substitute fresh names, should the persons receiving the panel feel that the list prepared by the Convenor was unduly biased or subjective. The Convenor would be bound to maintain all records of the exchange between him and the Eminent Hundred. Transparency in the process of selection of the Eminent Hundred, the panel of fifty names submitted to them for indicating their preference for the Governing Council, as well as the final list of the first Governing Council would be an essential element in maintaining the credibility of the model. The Eminent Hundred who would be the real initiators of the process of restoration of good governance can themselves be selected in several ways: by polls conducted by all the better known polling agencies in the country in a random survey and by then taking the names which are generally common to all the surveys; by asking all the national daily newspapers to request their readers to send their choice of the Eminent Hundred (or as many names as they can think *of)* and then nominating a team to select the names which are most common, in a transparent process; by asking chancellors of all the regional universities to go through a (somewhat) similar process and by then synthesising the same at the national level by an Academic Council; by establishing a process of this nature under the aegis of respected (retired) Justices of the Supreme Court and/or the High Court; or by any other process which will yield the most credible results while ensuring transparency. The members of the Governing Council and the Secretary

General will be changed every five years. After having served out their respective terms, none of these incumbents will seek any political office in the country for atleast five years. Nor will they function as appointees of the government in any capacity. The involvement of the core members of the MRGG has to be one of selfless dedication: in deed and in spirit.

The funding of the Movement will be entirely through voluntary donations. Transparency of accounts will be maintained at all times.

The path chosen by the MRGG for restoring the primacy of the rule of law and bringing in accountability will be through the exercise of a moral influence; of a dimension that will ensure that undesirable elements do not enter the political mainstream, either at the Centre or in the Provinces. It will exercise this influence (both by its moral standing as well as through the ballot) in any of the following ways: by supporting independent candidates who in its opinion best meet its criteria for clean politics; or, where it is not able to exercise the first two options, by backing the candidate coming closest to meeting such criteria, irrespective of party affiliations. Using its considerable prestige the MRGG will ceaselessly endeavour to promote public awareness and public insistence on clean politics and decorum in public life.

Policy guidelines, list of MRGG candidates, or candidates to be supported by the MRGG, will be approved by the Governing Council. The Council will also approve the expenditure estimates, put up to it by the Secretary General and review the balance sheets and auditor's reports.

The Governing Council of the MRGG (which will change every five years) will comprise eleven nationally respected figures from all walks of life, regardless of caste, creed or sex. A panel of fifty names for the first Council, for the years 1996-2000, will be prepared by the Convenor and circulated to 100 respected men and women country-wide to indicate their choice of eleven members, in order of priority. The result of the first selection by the Eminent Hundred will be announced publicly. No politician, past or present, would be eligible for membership of the Governing Council. For replacement Councils (every five years) a similar exercise will be undertaken by the sitting Governing Council six to twelve months before the date of change-over. A sitting Governing Council member would not be eligible for a second term. In the meetings of the Governing Council, each of the members will act as the Chairperson, in rotation, for the Council meetings. The sitting Chairperson will hold the function till the commencement of the subsequent meeting.

The first Secretary General will be the Convenor (founder) of the MRGG. He will hold this function till the year 2002. All subsequent Secretaries General will be appointed by the Governing Council for a five year term. No Secretary General may succeed himself. In case of ill-health or unsatisfactory functioning, the Secretary General may be replaced by a resolution passed by nine of the eleven Council members. The Secretary General will function as Chief Executive of the MRGG on behalf of the Governing Council and would be responsible for coordinating the day to day activities of the MRGG as well as for maintaining the accounts of the MRGG. The audit of MRGG accounts will be carried out annually by auditors appointed by the Governing Council. The audit report would be made available for public scrutiny. The Secretary General, at the time of accepting his mandate, would give a written undertaking to uphold the principles on which the MRGG is founded. He would also be responsible for preparing lists of candidates for election to the Parliament or Provincial Assemblies for approval of the Governing Council. Neither the Secretary General nor the Governing Council members would personally canvass for any candidate for any election or public office. The endorsement of the MRGG Governing Council for a candidate should, over a period of time, become synonymous with eminent suitability of the candidate in the public mind. The Secretary General will not exercise any voting rights in the deliberations of the Council.

Management of Funds

The MRGG will build a corpus by inviting donations from all individuals and bodies who wish to support the aims and objectives of the Movement.

The accounts will be audited annually by auditors appointed by the Governing Council. The auditor's report would be available for scrutiny to the public.

A Common Platform

The MRGG will initially field candidates for the Lok Sabha election who in the opinion of the Governing Council best fulfill the basic criterion of decency and selfless public service. MRGG members elected to the Lok Sabha, as distinct from independent candidates or candidates of other parties supported by the MRGG, will not aspire to any ministerial post. They will be expected to follow the guidelines laid down by the MRGG parliamentary leader who would be nominated by the MRGG Governing Council.

Should the MRGG be unable to field its own candidate or back a suitable independent candidate, it may elect to back any contender from any party provided that the MRGG Council is satisfied, that even if the candidate does not subscribe fully to the aims and objectives of the MRGG, backing the individual would perhaps defeat a rival candidate whose presence would vitiate the atmosphere of the elected body.

The support provided to the candidates selected for backing by the MRGG could be in the form of financial support or endorsement of the candidate, thereby putting the prestige of the MRGG behind the candidate.

The MRGG will not set up a party machine by enrolling party members in the manner of other political parties. It will set up regional committees for fixed terms in each district comprising volunteers who wish to support the aims and objectives of the MRGG. For the purpose of creating awareness, a massive media campaign will be launched with funds available to it through donations and by inviting citizens groups, environmental groups, NGOs and other like-minded people who wish to usher in an era of clean politics to canvass and work for the candidates selected by the MRGG council in that district.

Silent Majority

Many countries have been kept afloat not by their leaders but by the ordinary voter who has time and again shown maturity and sagacity and pulled the country back from the brink. Unfortunately, for that perspicacious voter his wisdom has not brought the amelioration sought by him due to the tenancious grip of malign elements on party machines and funds, both accounted and unaccounted. Politicians who have been voted out (or thrown out) keep re-emerging, never chastened by the previous debacle but having refined the process of self-aggrandisement. The voter does not really have a choice. He votes out one set of people and votes in the other lot simply as the lesser evil. The MRGG variant in politics could conceivably bring in that element of discrimination and choice.

2

INDIA – VISION AND REALITY

RE-APPRAISING THE IDEA OF INDIA

The 'Idea of India' has been variously commented upon by several persons, many of them well known, from the perspective of their own background, whether they be writers, expatriates, political scientists, constitutional experts, philosophers and the like. Almost invariably the discipline or the academic background of the person putting forward the ideas has manifested itself in the views expressed, perhaps naturally so. This point is mentioned because the diversity of views of the idea of India can be seen to be as abundant as the idea of India itself. On the academic plane, i.e., from the perspective of persons who are able to put across their views to a larger audience through their writings or discourses the 'Idea' has been regarded, or at times discredited as one or the other label, most notably cultural, civilisational, political or an amalgam of complexities, too difficult to discern with any degree of clarity. As if these complexities were not enough, the present dialogue on the idea of India has been overwhelmingly coloured by the controversy raging over secular and non-secular debates that have taken place or are taking shape at the very moment when the world itself is being buffeted by contradictions that it thought it had wound down for a century or more.

To a layman standing aloof from the debate on the idea of India, which itself is a subliminal thrust towards a perceived ideal for the person informing the debate, the idea per se becomes a superimposition of the beliefs or prejudices of the person concerned. Standing back, at some remove from a direct involvement, it should be possible for any objective observer to anticipate with a reasonable degree of accuracy the position likely to be taken by a well known person putting across his or her idea of India. This statement should not be construed as a criticism of a given mindset of the idea of India, which in several cases would be seen to conform to the ideal of the person formulating the idea of India. The digression at the start of the paper is made to show that the very subjectivity attached to the idea of India makes it an imperfect ideal for being accepted as such - in case it is meant to be so - by the majority of the people who go through the humdrum of Indian existence without trying to look for anything beyond the travails of their existence. To that extent the debate remains esoteric.

The amorphous nature of the idea of the 'Idea of India' allows for as many interpretations as there are people pondering over it as an intellectual exercise. There are so many ways of looking at a country whose civilisational base goes back to the dawn of civilization itself. An individual, or groups of individuals, who in their remoteness remain steeped in the traditions patterned on the lives of their forefathers since time immemorial do not have to delve into aspects that are of analytical, philosophical or historical interest to writers and savants, who debate these issues. They *live* the tradition. It is part of their very being. It is the continuum in their mind without a beginning, flows effortlessly into the present, and by their reckoning, moves as easily into the future. It is a faith and an understanding untrammeled by self-doubt or doubt about the tradition in which they are steeped.

There are others, comprising the bulk of the people of India, who may share the attitudes of their brethren, although the pre-modern type of existence would appear to be an anachronism to many people who have stepped into the modern world. Here again, by and large the new lifestyle adopted by them – by some as recently as the last 30 or 40 years – need not lead to questioning of their civilisational past or their idea of what that past was and how it is to be lived in the present. Therefore, in a statistical sense it would be only a small percentage of Indians who would be grappling with the question of what the idea of India represents to them or for them.

A re-worked idea of India, shaped at the beginning of the new century through the dizzying scientific break-throughs taking place at myriad points on the scientific horizon, must take into account the externalities that will have a major effect on the thinking of the Indian nation, of all nations, for that matter. True, that in a country like India the external impulses are felt most keenly, in the first instance, by the power elites and the globalised elites in the metropolitan cities most receptive to them. On the face of it they do not directly buffet the minds of people in communities still steeped in the ways of their forefathers. Although the trickle down effect is slower, much slower, it cannot be escaped altogether, even by people living in remote regions of the country, cocooned in their time warp due to their relative inaccessibility. Nevertheless, since the policies being enacted by the governing elites are directly influenced - or imposed upon - by the prime movers of globalisation they will, over a period of time, have an effect on the lives of most people; whether it would be to a lesser or greater degree will be determined by the distance of the communities from the centres of globalisation. Naturally, there will be other determinants as well.

Constitutional Vision

The India, which now situates itself at the dawn of the third millennium after Christ, must take into account the political aspect. Modern India, after attaining its independence in 1947 has been shaped, reshaped or become misshapen by the parliamentary form of government that the founding fathers of post-independent India chose for it in the belief that it represented the best ideal for 'their' idea of India; for transforming it, after centuries of subjugation, into a strong healthy society. Therefore, the country's political identity is based on its commitment to certain fundamental principles, namely justice, liberty, equality, fraternity and the dignity of the individual. Fundamental rights institutionalise, respect and protect the individual's dignity and freedom. The Directive Principles go further in that they have a strong egalitarian thrust. After 50 years of what many would call national decline, at least in the realm of governance, blame is being put upon the constitution, which India gave itself on achieving independence. Rightly or wrongly, whether condemning it outright or picking holes in it from time to time, it remains undeniable that the people at the helm of affairs who guided India's destiny through that turbulent period of the partition of India must have based their actions upon their idea of India. Something akin to what is being attempted now; except that in the present case the projections remain academic and possibly idealistic without the compelling burden of transforming those ideas into actions that could shape the country's future for the next 50 years or more, as was the case with the decisions that followed the ideation of the founding fathers of that earlier era.

It would be futile to keep harping on the rightness or otherwise of the decisions taken at that time by the leaders of the country whose stature and idealism as well as the sacrifices made by them during the freedom struggle conferred upon them an aura and mystique that few leaders can hope to achieve in the present day. Their stature as beloved leaders of their people reverberated beyond the confines of the India's geographic boundary. It cannot be a matter of satisfaction that charismatic leaders of yester years who rode as colossi on the national as well as global arenas have almost disappeared from the face of the earth, yielding place to pygmies who lead their people through autocratic dispensations or the vagaries of the ballot box. In the latter case, often coming to power for reasons far removed from their ability to lead their people.

Role of the Intelligentsia

Whether the Constitution failed India or the people who were in the ascendant over the years as educators, intellectuals, governing elites as well as the haves, failed the constitution and the country is a debate that is not likely to die down any time soon. Nor is it likely that the constitution, which for all its failings - real or imaginary - has become reasonably well embedded can be displaced or turned over in the foreseeable future. Fed up with the state of affairs, public ferment is bound to lead to changes, mostly for the good of the people as well as the country. Whether intellectuals and the educated elite, both within the country and the expatriates, will play a significant role as harbingers of salutary changes remains an open question. In the earlier centuries, men of letters influenced the thinking of their countrymen, or even the world, over long periods of time. In some cases the movement of ideas would be considered to have been glacial by present reckoning. This is where the most significant change has come in for the men of letters, the shapers of ideas, in the form of information technology. Hence, the ivory tower appellation of rarefied intellectual debates need not apply any longer, or at least not to the same extent. Diffusion and dissemination can take place very fast, with lightning speed if the mediums of transmission and diffusion happen to be receptive to the idea.

The political shape of the nation is bound to play an over-sized part – overwhelmingly larger, when compared to other factors that determine the future of the country. Ignoring this fact, building an ideal that does not take into account the ground reality in which India is anchored in the opening years of the 21st century, or mired as some others might like to word it, would make the idea devoid of substance.

Space For Religion and Gandhism

Two major streams that dominate the intellectual as well as political discourse of the country today relate to the place of religion in modern India and the relevance of the philosophy and ideals of Mahatma Gandhi. Coming first to religion, it was denied sufficient space in the political mainstream - as well as by officialdom - due to the political philosophy and the thinking of Pandit Jawaharlal Nehru, the first prime minister of India and the Congress Party that played an overarching role in the country's affairs in the opening decades after independence. Moreover, it might have been a conscious effort on the part of all concerned to exorcise the ghosts of the violent partition of India. Whether the post-secular society that India became in the last decades of the 20th century was inevitable on account of the transformations taking place in neighbouring countries and their influence on the two largest religious communities in India is a question that could be taken up by future historians. Whatever be the case, religion, in its more assertive and virulent form came up front in many parts of the world. India was no exception. Even if externalities had not impinged upon India, the country would have reached the same point, almost inevitably so, by a different route. If interdenominational clashes between the two main communities had not come to the fore earlier, it was also on account of the firm governance that obtained in the first few decades after independence, due as much to the latent stability resulting from over one century of strong, well regulated centralized authority in India. It was this latent stability, added to the competence and commitment of the leaders and civil servants who governed the country in the period immediately after independence that kept a lid on many of the ills seen raising their ugly heads today in the country. Matters, of course, came to a head during the emergency. The post-emergency decline in almost all spheres of governance and in almost all strata of society has led the country to the state that it finds itself in at the beginning of the new century. That it is not a happy state of affairs hardly needs reiteration.

The second important aspect relates to the philosophy of Gandhi. Although Gandhi continues to form an important part of the ongoing political and economic discourse taking place in the country, and elsewhere in the world for that matter, it has to be mentioned that in spite of the ideals of the Mahatma quoted with reverence at most forums discussing the future course of the country, his economic and political philosophy has not really found acceptance in the country, in so far as their practical application goes. And at the end it is difficult to think of an idea of India that completely dissociates itself from the maxims of the Mahatma, whether they relate to governance, sustainable development, harmony in pluralistic societies or for the conduct of nations in the global arena. It is not surprising that Gandhi continues to attract the attention of so many people around the world, both as the man and the ideals that he stood for. Unfortunately, the debate around the Mahatma rages, especially in India, around elements that were never put into practice in the land where they took birth.

Looking back on the events of the 20th century, both pre- and post-independence in India, one cannot fail to get the impression that although he did not lose hope or his faith in his ideals Gandhi might have died a disillusioned man. If not disillusioned, certainly heartsick at the turn of events. Did the bloodletting that took place at the time of partition in the land where for over four decades he had preached *ahimsa* (non-violence) indicate that his philosophy had failed? Amongst others, this was the land of Mahavira and Buddha. It did not end with partition. The bloodletting continues to this day, in every part of the subcontinent where the father of the nation travelled. If present indications are anything to go by it could continue well into the future seeing the current trends across national divides in all directions in the subcontinent. Hence, it can be seen that the ground reality is almost diametrically opposed to the Gandhian tradition that so many Indians continue to extol in public forums, be they intellectuals, social workers, politicians or economists. The ordinary Indian too continues to revere the memory of the Mahatma. When the state of affairs threatens to get out of hand people still go to Rajghat in ever increasing numbers to take a pledge at the *samadhi* of the Mahatma.

The increasing hiatus between Gandhianism and the policies followed by Gandhi's successors in India, regardless of their political leanings, raises fundamental questions for the idea of India. For the people of India, and for people around the world there can be no perception of India, real or imagined, where the ideals of the Mahatma do not loom large. How is this contradiction to be reconciled? Because, if it is not addressed and is merely glossed over at every public place within the country and without, where the name of Gandhi is taken, India will not be able to emerge unscathed from this troubling dissonance between the precept and its practice.

Seeing that India itself has veered so far away from the Gandhian mould it should have been possible to reject Gandhi's philosophy outright and move forward without a backward glance at an ideal that was considered impractical; or could not be put into effect in a land were shallowness, hypocrisy and untruthfulness have become the order of the day, at least in public life. In which case, getting rid of the baggage of Gandhianism and getting on with the governance of the country in the non-Gandhian mould that it has adapted should have been easy.

This has not been the case. At the same time untruthfulness and venality are in full cry the very leaders who have propelled the country in that direction have not been able to dispense with the trumpeting of Gandhi's legacy because of a lurking fear that should it be discarded India would not only have lost its way, it would have lost its soul. Then there would be no turning back. The thought of that final break, even shedding the pretence that is, troubles these people. They know that without the pretence they would not be able to face their countrymen, not at the hustings, not in public, possibly not even in private. At a deeper level they are not unaware that a final abandonment of

Gandhianism would be tantamount to condemning themselves to a karmic descent too horrid to contemplate. For, no matter how immoral the lot that governs the nation, in their heart of hearts they are deeply religious, albeit in a very warped sense of what their understanding of being religious should be. They also know that in India the vast majority of their countrymen revere the Mahatma and in spite of their poverty, deprivation and misery still closely adhere to the thoughts and ideals of Gandhiji. For, they are the ideals of Vivekananda, Sri Aurobindo and so many other sages and seers who moulded the character and destiny of India through the ages. That destiny that awaited India at midnight of 15th August 1947 has still eluded the country. Beneath the despair and turmoil that afflicts the land that destiny still awaits India. India has yet to produce the leaders who will take India to the pinnacle that the Mahatma and the sages before him dreamed of. And therefore, the ideal cannot be lost sight of. The ideal of Mahatma Gandhi is far too important for the redemption of India, if it is to find its feet and its true destiny. For the very same reason it is important for the world as well.

It is necessary to go a step further. The reasons as to why when the majority of Indians believe in it and the political leaders profess to believe in it, Gandhianism has not prevailed in the country of its origin have to be gone into. The main reason could be the difficulty of transplanting the Gandhian ideal of the early 20th century. Under an alien dispensation that ruled the country, and because of it being alien, it started uniting the country ideologically in the earlier decades before independence. The circumstances that obtained post-independence after the partition of India were not the same. And as the years went by, leading ultimately to the dominant market capitalist economy model pervading the world in the 21st century, the implementation of those ideas became even more difficult. Firstly, as mentioned earlier, the conditions had altered radically, and secondly, having moved so far away from the Gandhian philosophy and its economic derivatives it became increasingly difficult to retrace the steps taken. Having said that, the attempts at strengthening panchayati raj and the adherence to the principle, if not the practice, of sustainable development would qualify as a bow in the direction of Gandhianism.

Socialism to Capitalism

Meanwhile a fundamental change has taken place in the make up of the people of India – and the world as well. More than fifty years after Gandhi's death, the capitalist model – and the morality that goes with it - have become the norm. Even countries most staunchly opposed to it earlier, have embraced it whole-heartedly, notably Russia and China. Could people of those days when Gandhi was popularising the charkha have anything in common with Deng Xiaopeng's famous exhortation to his countrymen that, 'it is glorious to be rich'. If it is glorious to be rich, then there is nothing left of the Gandhian philosophy. If not the masses, at least the political class and the elites of modern India have embraced Deng's dictum as fervently as the Chinese in Beijing, Shanghai and Guangdong, in most cases as strongly as the Americans themselves. Whatever be the reason for this departure from socialism to capitalism, it is undeniable that going back to the economic idealism contained in Gandhi's writings would relegate India to an economic abyss from which there would be no recovery in the world of today. May be, when consumerism that is fast overtaking the globe makes life itself unsustainable on the planet, people across the world will start reappraising the economic philosophy of Gandhi. That is why the world is not going to forget Mahatma Gandhi. By association India, rightly or wrongly, will benefit from that grand reversal, whenever it takes place on a global scale. If India is to remain as part of the global economy, without completely shedding some of the desirable aspects of its socialist past, it must start its own reappraisal for benefiting from the vision of Gandhi wherever it is possible to transform that vision on the ground under the prevailing conditions in the country and the world. If the world has to save itself from self-destruction Gandhian non-violence must become the leitmotif of a globalised world, and a reformed UN structure that allows non-violence between states to become the norm for the 21st century.

It was possibly Mahatma Gandhi who said: 'for my worldly needs my village is my world; for my spiritual needs the world is my village'.

Indian Diaspora

The Indian diaspora is playing a much bigger role in moulding India's selfhood than it did before the 1990s. There could be several reasons for the renewed interest and what is more the new activism of the Indian expatriate community, which is now far more affluent and self-assured than their counterparts who left India to seek their fortunes in other lands before and after India's partition. The self-assurance and higher incomes have allowed people of Indian origin from around the world to participate more directly in India's development. The pace at which the interaction is taking place could have, over the ensuing decades, a positive effect far out of proportion to the strength of the Indian diaspora that is actively engaged in the exercise to move India forward. More importantly, the Indian diaspora is making itself heard in safeguarding the country's interest in the corridors of power in USA and elsewhere. The idea of India of the expatriates is in many ways distinct from that of their fellow Indians, in India. It is born out of their need for self-assertion in their adopted countries in a world where civilizations appear to be actually clashing - with the attendant uncertainties that such clashes generate for non-local persons.

The image of India for consumption in the West, notably America, as well as for consumption in India is also being shaped by Indian expatriates who now number in the tens of millions and whose wealth has grown into several billions of dollars. Their writings, actions and interactions have left an indelible impression on India's image abroad. The new lot of expatriates that went out to find their fortunes in the West after the information technology revolution represented a different breed from those that had gone earlier. The latter day emigrants being largely the products of prestigious Indian institutes started off at higher base income levels and quickly rose to prominence in several fields. For the same reason they were far more self-assured, articulate and conscious of the need to rebuild India, as well as to refurbish its image. Their common institutional backgrounds allowed them to network far more effectively than their predecessors. Networking allowed them to form pressure groups for influencing policy and thinking about India in the countries of their adoption. This cohesion did not go unnoticed in India, by the government of India, the political parties, the states, as well as the Indian media. In-country networking led to inter-country networking. As their self-confidence grows, along with their ability to influence developments in India, it suggests that the Indian diaspora will continue to play a significant role in the years ahead in remoulding India's image. Over a period of time this interaction between India and Indian expatriate communities is bound to enrich India in several ways.

When one speaks of global projection of the idea of India, there is a dual purpose attached to the idea of India. Firstly, it refers to the idea, which harmonizes with the idea that the Indian diaspora have formed and are propagating. It has to be dynamic. It cannot be something that is congealed in some hoary past and frozen at a given point in time, to be resurrected for showing India in a better light than the situation in the country at the dawn of the new millennium would warrant. Similarly, an idea of India that is superlatively formulated to show India as the repository of all earthly wisdom from time immemorial, to the exclusion of the contribution made by other civilizations would be at variance with the true spirit of the very wisdom that is being extolled. Arrogance, be it intellectual or on account of a great heritage, would not go down well with other components of the human mosaic of the 21st century. Therefore, the other aspect of the image that India wishes to transmit to the world must bring out the harmonising effect of the ancient message that travelled from India to many parts of the world before many of the world's religions in the ascendant today had come into being.

India will not be able to find its true identity or realistically arrive at an idea of itself, which the country can live comfortably with, as also make it a worthwhile idea for global projection unless the internal contradictions that are coming up are first addressed.

Impact of Technology

No set of people can really live in isolation or remain indifferent to the crosscurrents being generated in the globalised world. The advance of technology will soon invade every remote niche that remains in the world, be it spatial, in the geographical sense, or the privacy of the human mind, in the metaphysical sense. Hence, seeing the pervasiveness of the processes that are being mobilized for invading the last bastions of the human as well as the natural environment it would be appropriate to look around the world to see whether there is any country whose society can be seen, or can be deemed to be progressing towards the ideal state that a conclave of this nature would be attempting to interpret, or define, even if it were to remain a process of mere intellectualisation, at some remove from the practicality of the ideal sought.

Who shapes the national - and international - dialogue? It is an important question, because it is those people who have gathered unto themselves the instruments for shaping the dominant discourse of today, who are leading the world into the cul-de-sac of negativism and violence. When scanning the global horizon in pursuit of seeking out societies that may be headed toward an idea of an ideal state that comes nearest to the global ideal of the 21st century, one finds that wherever one looks, be it USA, Russia, China, the countries of Latin America, Africa, Asia or Europe, it is seen that almost all these societies have developed into systems that have been unable by and large to maintain or improve upon the social cohesion of societies, which is fast breaking down in most parts of the world. There are many factors that are leading to the fragmentation of stable or relatively stable systems - and societies - that had enjoyed a greater measure of peace and harmony than they do now. Whether the state of churning or flux has been brought on by the post-World War II, followed by the post-Cold War reordering of the world order, or as byproduct of rapid modernisation and globalisation, is a question that can be debated at length. Whatever be the case, the ambient condition today within societies – and between nations - is far from harmonious. Nor, on the face of it, does it seem to be heading in a direction that could bring comfort to people or nations.

The questions that would be uppermost in one's mind when contemplating India's future must take into account some, if not all, of the aspects that are tabulated below:

Has the political self-assertion, or the attempt at self-assertion by some of the deprived segments of Indian society now finding political representation, ameliorated the condition of these classes as a whole or has it merely enabled the new leaders of the backward classes to exploit the situation for their own aggrandisement at the cost of their communities, without bringing any real benefits to the latter? Carrying this thought process further, 'will these new leaders be co-opted into the governing elites once the process of self-aggrandisement has reached levels that allow them to emulate the sections that they were agitating against'?

What will be the outcome a few years hence of the metropolitan elites around the world consciously collaborating with the forces of globalisation? These forces might have started from America. However, they are no longer limited to that country. Leaders of political struggles, revolutionaries, upholders of public morality, social scientists and many others in similar categories have sought to describe their struggle or movement as one of liberation. It can be argued that the phrase 'struggle for liberation' has fallen into disuse, or become hackneyed. Nonetheless, it may become necessary to have another look at these cliches. Since they served their purpose admirably in the past, are they still relevant or do they sound hollow? Hollowness can result from overuse or misuse or it can be the result of the quality or worth of the people who use these slogans for purposes that may be far removed from the ideology that they proffer. At the end of it all when applying the term liberation to India, some clarity must obtain as to where the process of liberation would lead i.e., liberation from or liberation to? What the people are being liberated from has been variously described as hunger, want, deprivation, marginalisation, humiliation and all the ills that are visited upon the proverbial have-nots anywhere in the world. 'Liberation to' in its ideal sense can best be described in Tagore's immortal poem, which reads:

> Where the mind is without fear
> and the head is held high,
> Where knowledge is free,
> Where the world has not been broken
> Up into fragments by narrow domestic walls;
> Where words come out from the
> depth of truth;
> Where tireless striving stretches its
> arms towards perfection;
> Where the clear stream of reason
> has not lost its way
> into the dreary desert sand of dead habit;
> Where the mind is led forward
> by thee into ever-widening thought and action -
> into that heaven of freedom,
> my father, let my country awake.

All countries have their religious practices, faiths and beliefs. The distinctiveness of India lies in the primacy attaching to the concept of self-abnegation and self-denial. In many ways it goes deeper than similar tendencies that manifest themselves in many other religions and countries. It is for this reason that absolute poverty cannot be assigned a true statistical value in India. Because, at any given time, it is difficult to guess as to what percentage of the poor follow a lifestyle, which can be deemed to be below the poverty line due to circumstantial indigence, or the state of poverty being induced volitionally. It is practically impossible to fathom the number of mendicants who go around the country because they have chosen to adopt that particular way of life. Similarly, stories are still heard of well-to-do people giving up their wealth, finishing their duties as householders, and retiring to the banks of the Ganges to pass their remaining days in prayer, fasting, meditation and the like.

Most religions in the world, if not all of them, stress on the need for forgiveness, tolerance and compassion. In India compassion extended to all living beings. Many followers of Jainism to this day go to great levels to ensure that no harm comes to other living creatures. Compassion for all beings must remain at the forefront of societal activity and, when the country is strong enough, even form part of India's relations with other nations.

When looking at the tragedy unfolding in the Middle East and the region on account of the unilateral US intervention, shedding at some stage even the fig leaf of justification, for occupying Iraq the supine-ness of the leaders of the countries opposed to the intervention has to be examined. This is especially so in the case of India. In spite of the widespread anger against the Anglo-American intervention, the government chose pragmatism as the state response to the tragic event. Although the government's response was in conformity with the response of practically all the governments in the world that chose to play it safe, the issue is raised in this discussion because it is in juxtaposition to the idea of India, which leaders of India after independence have been propagating to the world. Although the world has long become weary of the sermonising coming from Indian shores, the message that came through was that India was a country that cherished the ideals of rightness of action and rightness of response. In abandoning its core values - the idea of an ancient civilization, steeped in wisdom and conscious of the difference between right and wrong - as a basis for conduct of foreign policy, the governmental elite of the country has vacated the space for basing international relations on the higher plane of moral principles to non-governmental entities or individuals who might command a measure of respect in public life. Needless to add that such abandonment of the path, or even the pretence, of right conduct, is in conformity with the prevailing norm across nations as the forces of globalisation infuse the world with their non-virtues or the pleasure principle as the fulcrun of all actions.

Years of Promise

To project or even propel India into a future which many people view with trepidation one must look over one's shoulder into the past. Not that remote past from which many people today want to draw their inspiration - more consciously than the ordinary consciousness that inheres in the minds of most Indians as to what that past might have been. That would be going too far back. Here, the past merely refers to the period after independence, divided into those early years when many of the participants (at the discussion) were very young, the Republic of India even younger. How did people of this generation look at India at that time, as it was unfolding in the ever present and flowing into a future that beckoned enticingly, even enchantingly. Doubtless there were difficulties, trials and tribulations, which the nation was undergoing. Whatever may have been happening, dejection and despair were not in the ascendant to the same level that they are today. A few decades on, having journeyed with

India into the new century, the same generation has a different vision of India. In spite of the remarkable progress made in many fields - and the achievements are certainly there for everyone to see - the spirit that pervades the nation seems to have lost the freshness and innocence, perhaps naivete of those early years. What India has evolved into in the first decade of the new century is certainly not in keeping with the vision of what India should have evolved into that people in the first decades after independence cherished.

Here we come to the first dissonance. India has gained in many respects. In several other ways India has declined. How does one strike a balance between the gains and losses when the gains are in the material plane and the losses in planes other than material. Care is being taken to avoid the use of the word spiritual when chalking up the gains and the losses. For while efforts to resurrect the hoary past merge into the realm of the spiritual, the understanding of spirituality obtaining now in India - and perhaps the rest of the world - is not the same as it might have been when the great Vedic hymns to creation were being first sung on the banks of sacred rivers that now stand as polluted as the spirits of the souls that still ritualistically immerse themselves in these flows to seek salvation. Looking at it this way, the foremost image that leaps to the surface in the consciousness plane of the beings of today is a vast sea of pollution where the scum that rises to the surface represents, symbolically, the spiritual progress, even if it cannot be measured so as to be able to offset it against the material gains; represented almost exactly on the day of the discourse by a figure of billion US dollars (represented on the basis of the foreign reserves of the country).

Where does one go from here? Should the country pitch headlong into the globalising mainstream and let the currents carry it in the direction of the new forms of nirvana, attained by the leaders of globalisation - the USA and the West, ably followed by their counterparts in the extreme east, China and Japan. Following the leader, in the true spirit of globalisation and the direction in which it is headed, will prevent people in India from falling between two stools, in this world and the next. The dilemma is very real. There are no easy answers. Having said that, answers have to be found. For it is not a question of black and white, of simply tossing a coin and then following the path indicated by the upward face of the coin, pointing towards the sky, the sun and the stars. It may be easier for other countries to do so, like China has done. India's manifest destiny does not lie in that direction. It lies in realms that can never be reached by true practitioners of globalisation. Writing in *The Hindu* (October 1, 2002), Naresh Gupta aptly sums it up when he states: "the world of today has achieved much, but for all its declared love for humanity, it has based itself far more on hatred and violence than on the virtues that make man human".

There is a need to engage with those who belittle and condemn India, so that their varied and rich talent does not remain tied to an acerbic condemnation of their country - no matter how real their concern - in a language that can only be appreciated by the educated elite and foreigners who joyously lap up this condemnation and confer great honors upon the authors. Condemnation for the sake of condemnation no matter how beautifully expressed is not likely to lead to any real amelioration of the conditions that gave rise to the anger or the condemnation. Writing in *Young India* in 1929, Mahatma Gandhi said: "My mission is not merely brotherhood of Indian humanity... My patriotism is not an exclusive thing... The conception of my patriotism is nothing if it is not always, in every case without exception, consistent with the broadest good of humanity at large." Rabindranath Tagore said that while nationalism was often a blessing, too often it has been a curse. The Indian philosophy of *Vasudaiva Kutumbakam* promotes the feeling of 'one world'. Jawaharlal Nehru propounded the concept of 'Panchsheel' as the basis of mutual relationship. The Bhagvad Gita and the Isavasyopanishad tell us that the yogi sees himself in all beings and all beings in himself. He sees the same in all. If one sees all living things as if they were in his body i.e. feels their joys and sorrows as his own, and sees the same Universal Spirit in all things then there is no need for protecting oneself against others. When a man understands that all beings are, indeed, the all-pervading Spirit, then he realizes the oneness of all things.

Whatever be one's station in life - from those who are below the poverty line to those who are the wielders of power-all need to be reminded that the primary status of everyone in the country is first and foremost that of a citizen. In that respect, all are coequal. Similarly, the comity of nations will have to push towards a United Nations dispensation wherein from the most deprived nations barely existing as civilized structures owing to over-exploitation and marginalisation, to those mighty nations who decide what is good for the world, all must strive for the democratization of the UN. Therefore, in reshaping the idea of India, its leaders have to recast their philosophy. They must resume engagement with all those who were being referred to as the 'third world' countries. The concept of the third world can be redefined to embrace all deprived nations whose primary impulse is towards global stability and harmony. In an over-exploited world these are mostly nations who are struggling to simply find a place in the sun. The idea of leadership itself must undergo fundamental transformation. Traditionally, when talking of a leadership role amongst nations, the implication was to unite the group to confront other groups of nations seeking dominance in some form or the other. That remained the mindset of the post-colonial era after World War II, when the marginalized nations of the world were trying to position themselves as a third force between the two superpowers of the day.

Virtue of Self-Denial

The 21st century reality of the unipolar world does not confer any leadership role upon India, should the country remain wedded to the prejudices of its earlier experience. If

India wants to be heard, if it wants to strike out independently for charting a course that propels the world away from confrontation and the growing spiral of violence, it must adopt, as a nation, the values that enriched India in the past and continue to enrich mankind wherever those values take root. Simply put, those values relate to non-violence and self-abnegation. The aspect of non-violence has already been touched upon. The point at issue now is, as to whether self-abnegation or self-denial, the greatest of human virtues in an individual can be extended to a nation. If the course of the history of violence since the last century, added to the proliferation of weapons of mass destruction is taken as a guide, the answer must be in the affirmative. There does not seem to be any other way. India is ideally positioned to take the lead. It must continue to make economic progress and strengthen itself internally and externally. However, having achieved these goals it should deny itself a position at the top table. It should not hanker after a permanent seat in the United Nations Security Council, as that body is presently structured. India should categorically state that it remains anchored to the aspiration of all third world countries that are looking to change the lot of their people; be they mired in backwardness and poverty because they were the victims of exploitation in the colonial era, or on account of misgovernance. Having been a part of the third world, India must seek a collective betterment for all the nations who comprise the vast collectivity known as the developing nations. Either they all benefit from the new dispensation, even if it were to be so incrementally, over a given period of time, or they collectively hold out for a more just world order. India must assure them that it will not desert them no matter how tempting the offers from the rich man's club. In reshaping the idea of India the individual and national identity must aspire to march together for a better self and a better world.

When picking up a daily newspaper at random in any of the metropolitan cities on any given day the impression is likely to remain that India is an aggregation of dissonances.

The images that flicker across the reader's perceptual frame could include: unity in diversity in juxtaposition to increasing disunity - the more the diversity, the greater the disunity; national integration opposed by national dis-aggregation; cultural plurality yielding place to cultural segregation; multi-ethnicities leading to multitudinous divisions; and now at the beginning of the new century the overarching intrusion of capitalism in full cry, which in developing countries like India translates into the accentuation of the divide between the haves and have-nots. It hardly needs to be stressed that for India to move ahead it needs to rededicate itself to the ideas of social justice, equality, fraternity, individual liberty and human dignity that were so well set out in the preamble to the Constitution of India.

People who gather together to talk about the idea of India or write about it, wherever they might happen to be have to think about providing a set of guidelines, if not answers, for the new generation growing up at the beginning of the 21st century to shape the future of India. The questions that they would be grappling with would include, inter alia:

* How much has the globe impinged on India?

How much is India impacting the world?

What do the young people of India want?

What questions are they posing?

What is our response?

Do we have a response (to their questions)?

When we write about these matters or articulate them in different forums in India and abroad whom are we targeting?

What audience is it actually reaching?

In the land of tolerance isn't it strange that discussion on tolerance has become one of the hottest issues?

Role models. Who are they?

Who or what represents the essence of India?

For whom?

India's conscience. Who are its minders and keepers? Do we really need minders and keepers?

Whatever the transformation in recent years and regardless of the polarization between religions and ethnic divides that is taking place, humaneness as the deeper instinct prevails more in Indian society than in many other societies. For example, the type of mass exterminations which were carried out during the Muslim invasions in many parts of Asia and during the era of the Christian colonization of the world, have never been attributed to Indian expansionism. Even the atrocities attributed to Indian security forces pale in comparison when compared to the scale of the atrocities committed by the armed forces of other nations. Any number of examples can be given: Pakistan, in East Bengal where the Pakistan army slaughtered three million people and raped half a million women, all of them Pakistan citizens since East Bengal was still a province of Pakistan when these atrocities were committed; the US excesses in Vietnam; the Chinese excesses in Xinjiang and Tibet; and so on.

At the dawn of the new millennium, when one looks around, it becomes abundantly clear that the spiral of violence within societies, and between nations, has reached self-energizing momentum that might only be stilled by a cataclysmic event, the likes of which has not been witnessed before in human experience.

Between societies and groupings that cohere to form nations the ideal situation that must be worked towards would be one where the need for primacy does not arise. Non-violence appears to be the antithesis of the global reality in today's world. Nevertheless, the concept of non-violence which is deemed to be the most profound contribution that ancient Indian thought made to the world must regain its primacy, within India and without, if human society is to continue to live in a civilized form. That the essential harmony of all sentient beings, indeed sentience itself, as put forward by Mahavira, Gautama Buddha and many others as the basis for India's freedom struggle by Mahatma Gandhi should not be looked at in isolation, as a mere reiteration of non-violence. By introducing the ancient precept into the mainstream of the anti-colonialism struggle in India, Gandhi may have been looking well beyond to the universal projection of his innate belief in the virtue of non-violence as a survival imperative for humanity, just when scientific breakthroughs were on the verge of putting immensely destructive capabilities into the hands of mankind.

Based on paper presented at the Rajiv Gandhi Foundation, New Delhi in May 2003.

INTERNAL THREAT TO INDIA'S DEMOCRACY IS LOOMING LARGER WITH EACH PASSING DAY

A few months ago a talk was delivered at the India International Centre on the theme "Is the Constitution Being Constitutionally Undermined"? The talk was well-received by the distinguished audience present. Seeing what has been happening in the country in the ensuing months and the steep decline that has set in, practically across the board, the remarks made were not wide off the mark.

It is not hard to notice the 'constitutional undermining' of the constitution that is taking place in full public view and the erosion of the 'right to equality' before the law that is being jeopardised by the very bodies - the parliament and the executive - that should be the principal upholders of the rule of law. That they are not is no longer in doubt. In fact, it can be shown that the legislators and the governing machinery have become the principal violators of the law of the land. A large number of them seem to be leading the charge in the breakdown of democracy and law and order for the ordinary citizen, i.e. for the common man in India.

A news item appeared recently with the title 'Trainee sub-inspector transferred for misbehaving with politician' (*The Sunday Express*, September 12, 2010, Page #4 Delhi Newsline). It is not an isolated case. Many people have been privy to a number of similar cases that go unreported. In the prevailing conditions in the land there is little likelihood of a police trainee constable or officer having the temerity to check these high level violators of the law. Should a conscientious police functionary demonstrate the courage to check any legislator, leave alone executive of the government, he would be given short shrift. Again, many such instances have been reported over the years. Honest police personnel are a demoralised lot. Several years ago there was a case in Meerut where a police constable detailed specifically to check all persons attending a meeting (possibly of the Chief Minister) was sent back to the lines and possibly dealt with severely thereafter for asking to see the identity papers of a person who happened to be a minister from the minority community. The latter had complained to the CM. The result is that national security stands compromised. Many terrorists get away by flashing red lights on their vehicles or posing as legislators (who have become the terror of the state police), because the policeman posted to check that no suspect gets through would rather play safe. Such lapses would simply not be permitted in most other countries.

The first line in the fight against terrorism is the policeman. In a district the most important functionaries are the district magistrate and the SSP. It takes minimum one year to get the feel of the district, after which suitable steps can be taken by the incumbents to strengthen intelligence and plug loopholes through which anti-social elements and elements inimical to the country often get through. When transfer of these incumbents, who are the cornerstone of good order, security of the district and sound administration, is effected at the whims and fancies of every new CM and lately at the instance of the 'bahubalis' and known criminals (who have become legislators and ministers), good order, discipline and basic governance for the ordinary citizen stand crippled. A body blow is being routinely administered to democratic functioning. The time for weak admonitions is past. The Courts have to step in decisively to preserve democracy. They represent the last hope for the suffering public.

In like fashion, if the CBI and sister agencies, who are the watchdogs of society, are treated like lapdogs of the power coteries that have taken over the reins of government, national security is threatened more ominously from internal rather than external sources. It is elementary that when thousands of crores of rupees are siphoned off no one individual can indulge in the scam singly. Several subordinates, even colleagues would be in the know, might even have abetted in it or shared in the loot. Hence, the concerned administrator, minister, chief minister or higher ups in the Centre would be amenable to exposure and blackmail.

Several decisions would be taken to keep the blackmailers off their backs. Similarly, a number of foreign governments are aware of the identity of the holders of the funds placed illegally in foreign banks and the lists that are now floating about or have been made available to the government. With the CBI and tax agencies corrupted or subverted (such being the public perception), prosecution is held up within the country. It suits the foreign governments admirably. They can then safely continue to indulge in the blackmail of the tainted leaders for longer periods or indefinitely and force them to take decisions that are not in India's interest. National security is being comprehensively jeopardised to a degree that is frightening. Yet, there is no relief in sight.

The point that is being highlighted is that very openly (*khul-e-aam*) the right to equality is being violated all the time in almost every part of the country by the discriminatory treatment being meted out to the ordinary citizen. It is not that the judiciary is unaware of the state of affairs in the country and the terminal degeneracy that has set in amongst large segments of the law givers and supposed upholders of the law, especially the agencies that are constitutionally required to uphold and 'respect' the equality of every citizen before the law.

That is not all. The biggest travesty is that the higher or the very highest level law breakers, who are now well above the law, claim special privileges and dispensations as *representatives* of the people. The fact that many of them are known criminals is hardly the point. Today the vast majority of the legislators, and large number of ministers, the famous 'executive' in the latter case, do not represent the people, or anybody for that matter, except those who appointed or anointed them. In the first-past-the-post system prevailing in India, the majority of the legislators have come in with very low percent of the votes, often as little as 10 to

20 percent or sometimes up to 30%. Ipso facto it can be inferred there from that 70% of the electorate in their respective constituencies *rejected* them. The bigger anomaly is that many aspirants for parliament *rejected* in the Lok Sabha election are appointed as ministers, even as prime minister or chief ministers (in the States), through the back door - or the Rajya Sabha route. What claim do any of these categories have to *represent* the people, act as law givers, or ride roughshod over the very agencies provided by the Constitution to protect the interest of the country and the common man. The public has come to the end of its tether, with no recourse in sight for amelioration of their condition.

In the light of the foregoing it would be in the fitness of things were the Supreme Court to take *suo motu* note of the destruction and demoralisation of the law enforcing agencies and the palpable violation of the constitutional right to equality being witnessed daily by the judiciary. At the very least the Centre and the States should be directed to give teeth to the Supreme Court direction on police reforms by a fresh date to be notified by the Supreme Court, but not later than 31st March, 2013, after which a constitution bench may be obliged to give firm direction to prevent a final breakdown of the democratic order in the country.

It is with deep anguish that civil society and concerned citizens, who have been battling for decades to prevent the country from going under due to the accumulated weight of corruption and violation of the law at the apex of governance and down the chain of governance at the Centre and the States, approach the Courts for elementary security and equality before the law.

3

FALTERING GOVERNANCE

TURNING A BLIND EYE

If one takes the line of thinking opened up by the Honourable Supreme Court to its logical conclusion one comes up with the dreadful deduction that today the biggest threat to the security of India might be the political class, full 20 per cent of whose members happen to have criminal cases registered against them. If the percentage as given out by the Election Commission is right then the criminal class that has entered Parliament is perhaps one of the single largest blocks, although affiliated to political parties across the political divide.

Leaving the rest of the country to fend for itself the political class cocoons itself in the security provided by gun-toting bodyguards paid for by the exchequer, irrespective of whether the persons so protected have a number of murder, dacoity or rape cases pending against them. Indian democracy is definitely on the march, in all its glory. The march is toward the abyss. In all other countries the political class comes together in the face of national emergencies. In India they come together to undermine the decisions of the highest judicial bodies in the country. In no other country in the world are the decisions of the Supreme Court– the final arbiter – overturned or thwarted as summarily as is presently happening in India.

The earlier figures relating to criminals as legislators were already alarming. The latest figures available for the election in UP indicate that the biggest parties contending the polls have given tickets to a larger number of candidates with criminal background, many of whom are notorious history-sheeters. They terrorise the people, having committed many dacoities, rapes and murders. That is not all. A large number of candidates given tickets by these parties have shown assets running into crores of rupees in the affidavits filed by them. They have not given their PAN identifications. It would mean that they do not file income tax returns or that they are shielded by the powers responsible for prosecuting them.

The famous 'tipping point' was crossed long ago. If one logically follows the graph of the entrants into the national parliament and the legislative assemblies the curve is likely to show the 50 per cent mark being crossed any time in the next 10 to 15 years. It means that by the years 2015-2020, India and a large number of states of the Indian Union would comprise legislators, the majority of whom would have criminal backgrounds. Going by the current practice at least 30 per cent of them would then go on to hold ministerial portfolios at the Centre and in the States. So much for India being touted in global fora as the largest democracy in the world.

Leaving aside these self-evident and undeniable facts it can be easily demonstrated that terminal degeneracy has indeed set in, in many aspects of governance that affect the daily lives of the overwhelming majority of India's citizens. Ask the common man in UP, Bihar and in other states as to which enemy he/she fears the most. As often as not the answer would be, Saheb, Sarkar se Bachaiye", (freely translated it would mean, "Please save us from the myrmidons of tyranny"). And when you further question them as to who the myrmidons of tyranny might be, the answer is likely to be – the policeman, the corrupt bureaucrat, the local 'bahubali' (strongman) supported by the local legislator. In many cases the legislator with a criminal background is himself the bahubali, supported by the local thana (police station). Jointly they become the worst oppressors.

There is no exaggeration in what has been stated. This is the state of Indian democracy for a large majority of deprived Indians living away from media glare and mostly out of reach of any activism - judicial or otherwise. The political class, the so-called guardians of democracy have been the prime culprits in pushing the country to this national decline. (Of course there have been honourable exceptions). The political class instead of ameliorating the lot of the people whom it represents has generally enriched itself at their cost and provided itself with gun-toting bodyguards paid for by the state exchequers, depriving the ordinary citizen of elementary protection. Moreover, to perpetuate their hold they have exacerbated caste and communal divides in ingenious ways.

Even if one were to leave aside the abysmal lot of a large percentage of India's population and think of India's future in the face of the fast emerging global threats, what has the government done to face these challenges? A few well-documented and incontrovertible examples highlight the national decline. The government of India and the state governments have demonstrated their complete inability to save the flora and fauna of India - the forests are being decimated at an increasing rate. They are being poached routinely and repeatedly. For over 50 years the people have watched with amazement the government's infirmity in saving India's natural heritage, which among other things accounts for a number of tourists visiting India. In spite of spending thousands of crores of rupees the pollution levels in the Ganga and the Yamuna might actually have gone up. These two river systems are famous for a variety of reasons. Should similar surveys be undertaken for many other waterways and water bodies the state of decline would be seen to be far worse.

One can go on in this vein ad infinitum to show that laws are being flouted with greater and greater impunity, mostly by the legislators and people at the helm of affairs. 'Equality before the law' is more in the breach than in practice.

In this sea of dreariness and despair the higher judiciary holds out some hope for the people of India. If terminal decline has been arrested in certain areas of governance it is due to the yeoman service rendered by the higher judiciary - there have been and would always be some glaring lapses - and the Election Commission of India. They are beacons of hope for India and many other countries that have started looking towards India. There should be no doubt in the mind of the political class that the public at large overwhelmingly supports most of the judicial interventions undertaken in recent years at the highest levels. It is certainly not in the long-term interest of Indian democracy that the judiciary is brought into ridicule by all and sundry, especially the political class. It is because of the respect for the courts and the highest judicial bodies in the land that most of the political bahubalis- many with criminal backgrounds and disproportionate assets, occupying the highest ministerial posts in the states and at the Centre - have not been lynched by the public on demitting office or shot by law and order forces when called in to restore order every time there is a breakdown in law and order.

The political classes beware. Do not gang up to undermine the judiciary. It is because of them that many of you continue to enjoy ill-gotten gains. Should you bring down the edifice you will be the worst sufferers.

FUNDAMENTALS OF GOOD GOVERNANCE

You would recall the **Model for Restoration of Good Government,** unveiled at a talk delivered at the India International Centre on 21 Oct 1995. The Model has universal applicability, wherever democracy is threatened with terminal degradation. Eminent persons and concerned citizens from many places have sent in very useful comments.

After several articles appeared in the national dailies (copies enclosed) there was an insistent clamour for implementing the Model i.e., it should move from the seminar stage to the grass roots. This takes on added urgency in the light of the latest developments in the country. The majority of politicians and leaders stand tainted. With their credibility at rock bottom they are sure to be wiped out. If nothing is done to provide credible alternatives a **coup de grâce** will be delivered to Indian democracy. One bunch of no-gooders will be replaced by another. Hardly a promising prospect.

In the light of the foregoing it is planned to launch the Model - almost exactly on the lines mentioned in the text, with minor modifications necessitated due to shortage of time. However, there will be NO deviation from the basic tenets: the Convenor and the Governing Council of the Movement for Restoration of Good Government (MRGG) must not themselves aspire to any political office - they must adhere to the self-destruct mechanism of the Model in the given time frame; and absolute transparency must be maintained at all times.

A summary of the **"national agenda"** which will guide the MRGG in the selection (or backing) of candidates is given below:

- Promoting effective governance at all levels by excluding political interference in the day-to-day work of the civil services and law and order forces.
- Upholding the principle of accountability at all levels of governance.
- Support of public action litigation by concerned citizens' action groups.
- Supporting special legislation for the removal and prosecution of corrupt Ministers.
- Strengthening the agencies for effective monitoring and **protection of the environment.**
- Eschewing caste-based politics and communalism in any form by upholding the spirit of the Constitution.

- Greater transparency in the government's functioning in areas not directly related to national defence and state security.
- Security of tenure of civil servants.
- Transparent procedures for the selection of the most competent persons (not necessarily bureaucrats) to head government enterprises and undertakings.
- The setting up of independent commissions for effecting transfers in the police and other enforcement agencies in line with the Police Commission report.
- **Population stabilisation as an overriding national priority.**
- Strengthening SAARC.
- Evolving a national consensus on vital issues related to India's long term security interests.
- Setting up of a properly constituted National Security Council.
- Creation of ombudsman.

Time is now of the essence. You are requested to please render all help to MRGG so that a credible alternative is provided to the people of India in the next hundred days or so before the Lok Sabha elections. A nucleus MRGG headquarters has been set up in New Delhi. Several eminent persons and concerned citizens are participating (in a self-effacing manner). They are not looking for any personal rewards at the end of the day; merely the satisfaction of knowing that they have contributed their mite to preventing the country from going into an irreversible decline.

At this juncture you can help in any of the following ways:

- Distribute copies of the Model to your friends, colleagues and employees. They must be made aware of the vital need for discrimination in casting their vote. If they send good people to the Lok Sabha in

1996 we are bound to see an improvement in the quality of governance in the country well before the turn of the century.

- The text of the Model to be (profesionally) translated into local languages for distribution to as many people as possible. (It has to be ensured that the printing or photocopying is of a good quality). A copy of the translation should be sent back to MRGG headquarters.
- Sending in suggestions for improving the quality and universality of the national agenda.
- Any other support or advice.

The MRGG is apolitical. To that extent, every citizen of the country who believes in INDIA FIRST - ALWAYS AND EVERY TIME or BHARAT PEHLE - HAMESHA AUR HAR WAKT, becomes a MRGG convenor.

In the belief that destiny still beckons.

MRGG QUESTIONNAIRE FOR POLITICAL PARTIES CONTESTING THE LOK SABHA ELECTIONS

On Good Government

1. Do you feel there is a need to improve the quality of governance in the country?
2. If so, what concrete measures do you propose in this regard? In what time frame?
3. Do you, in principle, accept the recommendations of the National Police Commission Report? What is your policy for their implementation? In what time frame?
4. Will you support legislation for the Lokpal Bill?

Population

5. Do you think population stabilisation needs to be given overriding national priority?
6. What specific measures will you adopt to give a fillip to population stabilisation?

Environment

7. Spell out the measures that your party proposes for effectively safeguarding the environment.
8. In what time frame will these be implemented?

National Security

9. Give out your party's policy statement on the important issues related to national security.
10. Do you support the setting up of an independent National Security Council?
11. If yes, in what time-frame? What will be its composition?
12. How will you ensure its effectiveness?

Criminalisation of Politics

13. Do you believe that people with a criminal record or those facing charges for grave offences should be given party tickets?

14. If not, what has your party done about it?
15. Have you given tickets to any persons falling in these categories? How many?

Accountability

16. What concrete steps will you take to ensure accountability for non-performance, or misgovernance, on the part of government servants and their political heads?
17. Do you believe that public sector enterprises should be efficiently managed by professionals (who can ensure their good performance and financial viability) for the benefit of the people or should these continue to be run as at present i.e. steeped in mis-management and financial irregularities?

Electoral Reforms

18. What are your party's views and stated policy on electoral expenses and other urgent electoral reforms?
19. What steps will you take to implement these refoms? In what time frame?

Transparency

20. Do you believe that there is need for greater transparency in government functioning in areas other than national security?
21. What steps will you take to bring about such transparency?

Women's Empowerment, Poverty Eradication and Education

22. What are your party's views on these issues?
23. If your party believes that they are important what specific, time-bound steps do you propose on each of these issues?

Downsizing in Government

24. Do you feel that the bureaucracy is bloated?
25. What measures for downsizing do you propose?

Creating National Harmony

26. What comes first? Your country or your party?
27. Spell out the measures that your party proposes for stengthening national unity?

March 1996

(Convenor MRGG)

REVITALISATION OF INDIAN DEMOCRACY*

Transitional Modes

Democracy in India is in a state of flux. Although conditions in many parts of the country are tending towards the anarchic, one would still hesitate to call it a state of chaos. If, in spite of constant buffetting, the edifice of democracy still holds it is only because some of the pillars that provide it foundational stability continue to be reliable. Hence, whatever means adopted to stem the rot in the body politic it has to be ensured that the pillars that provide it a modicum of stability are not allowed to be weakened any further.

In initiating the revitalisation process one has to proceed on the basis that the worst fears relating to terminal degeneracy in the body politic have not been groundless. Almost the entire process of governance at the political apex today seems to be concentrated solely upon devising stratagems to subvert the law and order apparatus of the state; to put a veil over misdeeds of the governing hierarchy of yesteryear. What a swansong for the party that comprised towering personalities of India's freedom struggle, among whom could be counted some of the most illustrious figures of the twentieth century. In the confusion thus created newer misdeeds are being piled on at a pace faster than the country's ability to deal with them. Intractable national problems crying out for immediate attention are glossed over in two line inanities in party manifestos just before elections. Hardly any political party seems to have any real idea as to how to address these problems. Whatever governance that is taking place is by default.

For several years, the process of governance has been terminally subverted. Many key appointments, including ambassadorial appointments, have been made with an eye to safeguarding the personal interests of one or two families. Had these appointees displayed the same zeal in safeguarding the national interest as they displayed in looking after the interests of individuals who have long ceased to be respected by the nation - many of them are actually despised - the country would not be in such dire straits today. These patterns too are being repeated, and condoned, in power centres developing elsewhere.

Stark as it may seem, the worst case scenarios flowing from such assumptions have the following connotation:

- The report by a Committee headed by an erstwhile Home Secretary on the political-criminal nexus was only able to look at the fringes of the problem, the nexus in actual fact, has penetrated so deep and extensively into the system that if would be "prudent" to assume that in many cases elements inimical to the state have assumed actual control of the levers of power. With such control they would be in a position to systematically thwart, at every stage, all attempts at reform.
- The principal organs of state security and governance stability have ceased to be accountable to any institution, body or process that "guarantees" the primacy of the national interest.
- A majority of the police departments and protection agencies of the government have reached such a state of terminal degeneracy that the normal remedies available in functional democracies to right the situation would no longer be efficacious.
- The sums of money available to the interests that threaten India's cohesion and governance stability are so large that an accurate analysis of their net worth could still send shock waves in a public innured to such revelations. (For a long time to come it may never be known whether a deliberate process of sabotage is under way when weak or clumsy chargesheets against suspected individuals are filed in the courts after months and years of preparation. "Is it a systematic sabotage of the Rule of Law?" Practices long prevalent in mofussil towns and state capitals, are now surfacing

in the Capital of India. These people are managing to kill two birds with one stone. On the one hand the public is informed that the law "will" take its own course. The high and mighty will "not" be spared. The high and mighty are named. Very few of them, in spite of the fanfare, are actually brought to book. Here an analogy from another part of the subcontinent may not be inappropriate. Kabul and some other Afghan cities fell without fighting. Money power tells. To what extent is it "telling" in Delhi?)

Unless one is "fully" alive to the seriousness of the situation all attempts at redressal are bound to fail. The crux of the dilemma can be stated simply: "barring the instrumentality of last resort (the Indian Army) almost all the instruments available to tackle terminal malignancies have either been blunted or are in the process of being blunted." The grimness of the situation gets magnified with the realisation that, in many cases, the instruments "themselves" have become the biggest threat to the security of the state and the well-being of the peoples. Should the present decline continue it could only be matter of time before the penultimate stage of structural collapse comes about. Put even more succinctly, that stage can be described as the state (in its partially commandeered form) versus the people of India. The resolution of the problem then lies in the ability of the revitalisation process to eject the undesirable elements who have commandeered (or crept into) key positions without irretrievably damaging the basic structure of the Constitution. (These elements generally stand exposed).

Ideally the situation could be remedied overnight by flooding the *sub rosa* domain of influence-peddling in the Capital with the light of total judicial exposure. By its nature this process is slow, conservative and cautious. The process has already started. It is irreversible. It is being hastened by the complete disregard of the national interest by the dying remnants of the ancient regime. The reprieve is temporary. The rout, when it takes place, will be absolute.

The electorate had already indicated its desire for change. The process will be completed well before the century is out. What has now to be ensured is that in the interim elements as degenerate as those being replaced do not move in to fill the vacuum. Change is inevitable; constant vigilance will ensure that the change is for the better. In order to prevent the Bihar model of governance from occupying the central space in India's polity anticipatory proposals that can be implemented without major constitutional changes should be considered at the earliest.

The title of the article suggests that Indian Democracy could be in a transitional phase. The pertinent issue here is whether the transition is towards a more degenerative state or it is the churning process that will usher in a just order. It is the latter process which will assert itself, if the enormous residual strengths of the nation are harnessed for strengthening the democracy. The old order is dying before one's very eyes. It is yielding place to the new. Hence, no tears need be shed for that which must wither away. One could go astray, however, in "rivetting" one's attention on the rotting corpse; thereby, failing to discern the long term trends - both degenerative and regenerative - which are manifesting themselves on the horizon. Briefly, the trends which can be clearly discerned are:

A tendency towards "warlordism". This is a direct result of fragmentation of the polity on caste and communal lines. In the most populous States the established law and order machinery is being deliberately destroyed by the political parties and subverted along parochial lines. Elsewhere, the formation of local '*senas*' is going unchallenged. The tendency must be nipped in the bud, without further ado, before the instrumentalities that can deal with them, "effectively and constitutionally", are weakened; as was attempted during the Emergency.

A strange reversal in the pattern of instability appears to be taking shape. For several decades after independence the rays of stability radiated from the heartland - the great Indo-Gangetic plain to the periphery. Today instability is increasing at the core while stability might start returning at the periphery. The prime role of the Indian army in restoring stability at the periphery, against overwhelming odds, must be taken note of; and this instrumentality of last resort strengthened as a high priority. Strengthening refers to an entire gamut of steps that must be taken urgently to restore the self-respect and self-confidence of the personnel of this magnificent, globally respected fighting force; and not merely an increase in the defence budget.

The "body" of the Constitution is being savaged at the hands of its prime custodians. The "spirit" of the Constitution is still alive. It is being kept alive by millions upon millions of ordinary law abiding citizens, conscientious civil servants, uniformed men, the press, the judiciary and countless others who greatly outnumber the handful of people in the first category. The spirit will prevail. The body will thereafter, be restored to health.

Awakening in Judiciary

The term "judicial activism" is a misnomer. The judiciary, media hype notwithstanding, has not been active. If the judiciary had really been active the daily charade being witnessed in this regard would not be taking place. This pillar of the Constitution too was sought to be emasculated during the Emergency and the decade which followed. The judiciary did not cover itself with glory in the intervening period. It was relatively inactive and pliable. It is only now becoming conscious of the enormous responsibility it shoulders for saving the Constitution from a polity which has gone berserk. Now that it is alive to the expectations of the people, and confident of the confidence that they repose in it, it is beginning to find its feet. Judicial activism has to begin now to restore the enormous damage to the collective national psyche.

Undermining of Merit

Meritocracy *is* being systematically destroyed in the country, mostly by people who should never have been anywhere near the process of governance, if democracy had found its moorings earlier. Excellence is being killed in academe, scientific bodies and almost every government department. Should a concerted effort not be made (by people who should know better) to halt and then reverse the trend, the situation could become irretrievable within a decade. A conscious decision will have to be taken by all concerned to resist unwarranted political interference. Two other measures will have to be adopted urgently to halt the drift to mediocrity; followed, thereafter, by imbecility. The measures relate to a decision by the Parliament, and if that body fails the judiciary, that with effect from 1 January 2000 the process of "de-reservation" will be set in motion. Progressively, all reservations under the existing criteria should be phased out by the year 2010. The polity, however, sees things differently. It seems to be bent upon creating further divisions in society. The vast majority of the classes who are supposed to be the beneficiaries never really benefit from ill-conceived reservation policies; which merely set in motion more vicious forms of sub-casteism and create new power centres for those who know how to manipulate the system. It is the ultimate in lack of accountability. Real empowerment can only be brought about by the improvement of education and health at the grass roots and the prevention of embezzlement, through draconian measures if necessary, of funds allocated for development and poverty alleviation. Governance, as well as the management of the higher institutions in the country, besides being extremely complex require considerable experience, skill and specialised knowledge. It mandates that the most talented people in the land manage such organisations. Elevating mediocre or semi-literate individuals on caste basis can never raise the standards of these castes. What will surely happen is that the national standards will go into an irreversible decline. Public Service Commisions, the Election Commision, Vice

Chanellors of central universities, heads of certain Public Sector Undertakings and all important agencies of the Goverment of India should be selected by impartial bodies, guided solely by the national interest and the ineluctable need for preventing further deterioration in standards. The President, or the highest Judicial body, should *suo motu* appoint such an impartial body, headed by a retired Chief Justice of the Supreme Court. The other members would comprise the leaders of opposition parties having not less than fifty elected members in the Lok Sabha, the Deputy Chairman of the Rajya Sabha, the Speaker of the Lok Sabha, the Home Minister, the Cabinet Secretary and the Secretary, Department of Personnel. Similar interim measures, limited to a period of ten years, could be adopted for the States.

The criminalisation of politics has been extensively covered in the media in recent years. Nevertheless, almost every political party unabashedly continues to field candidates with criminal backgrounds for election in greater numbers. Since the political parties are unable or unwilling, to check this grave threat to the democratic process the judiciary might have to impose an across the board injunction against such people to prevent them from standing for elections, with effect from the next general election. This could be an interim injunction for a period of ten years, or till such time Parliament is in a position to enact suitable legislation.

More and more political leaders are threatening to plunge their States in a bloodbath whenever their criminality stands exposed, or when their warlordism is checked, and while the law takes its lengthy course their henchmen play havoc with the lives and properties of their opponents. It behoves the nation to take up their challenge at the first utterance. Should the Parliament find it inconvenient to uphold the dignity of the Constitution then the Courts must intevene decisively. The public expects them to do so. The ordinary citizens are being killed, maimed and harassed in increasing numbers. An immediate stop must be put to this, by whatever means available.

Before suggesting any remedies it needs to be reiterated that the Constitution of India, in its essentials, is intrinsically viable. It is, all things considered, a workable Constitution. Where the framers of the Constitution made a gross error of judgement was in not being able to fathom the depths of venality to which the politicians who would follow the first batch of Gandhian leaders would be capable of sinking. Even in their wildest dreams the founding fathers could not have imagined the distancing that would take place between the Gandhian values of yesteryear and those of latter day politicians. It was an error of judgment that was to cost the country dear. Essential safeguards were left out in the belief that these would be incorporated as the wisdom of the polity improved over the years. These safeguards will have to be incorporated now.

A clamour is often generated for re-casting the Constitution or for a new Constituent Assembly. What many of the proponents of these demands do not seem to realise is that the members of the Constituent Assembly at the time of independence possessed a sagacity, maturity, stature and selflessness that can seldom be replicated in this day and age, in this country, or elsewhere. It would be worth remembering that were a new Constituent Assembly to take shape today its members might not measure up to the eminence, respectability and "universal acceptability" of the members of the first Constituent Assembly. Further, it becomes a moot point as to who exactly would nominate these members. Should a new Constitution be considered for India at some future date, the most appropriate time would be when the literacy level across the country embraces atleast seventy five per cent of the electorate.

Transparency, Decentralisation and Re-centralisation

There is a persistent demand all over the country for greater transparency and decentralisation. Justifiably so.

There is no denying the fact that democracy will be strengthened by more direct involvement of people in all parts of the country. This process is under way. It needs to be speeded up. Again, it has to be kept in mind that greater participation at the periphery does not necessarily mean the dismantling of agencies which, if well-handled, could actually strengthen participative democracy. Decision-making today is not as simple an affair as it was only a few decades ago. Sitting under the village banyan tree around a "*hookah*" might not always lead to wise decisions. At best, the village elders (if they have not been politicised along caste lines) can decide the priorities of development and help in ensuring that the funds reaching them are not mismanaged. The optimum utilisation of resources, however, requires skills, (and inputs) which at this stage of India's literacy and social development would neither be available at the village level nor fully grasped without benevolent expert advice. Hence, there has to be a drastic change in the mind-set of officialdom at higher levels. Besides ensuring complete transparency they have to be seen as welcome visitors, proferring unbiased advice.

It is in everyone's interest to decentralise - but imaginatively - in a manner where the ills that have overwhelmed society at the upper political and administrative levels are not visited upon the levels whch have yet to be empowered. It has to be a benign process. The Bihar model of governance should not become the norm for the country as a whole. The present situation, practically everywhere in the country, should not lead one to believe that the process which reins supreme at the apex is not being replicated at the grass roots. Doubters can visit almsot any backward area to verify for themselves the actual state of affairs where responsible social workers arc not present or the press is not vigilant (some of the innovative experiments in decentralisation now being tried out in Kerala and elsewhere are a step in the right direction).

Development processes everywhere in the world are becoming more interactive and complex; often due to reasons beyond the control of local inhabitants. Conversely, their activities, if not monitored from a larger perspective could, over varying periods of time, have deleterious effects beyond their horizons - of geography, perspective and development. Global environmental standards, hereafter, will require far more drastic supervision (and centralisation) than ever before. This is true both at the country and global planes.

India is blessed with a Constitution that gives sufficient powers to governance centrality to tackle the almost insurmountable problems of tomorrow looming over the global horizon of every nation, and mankind as a whole. It has taken nearly half a century of painstaking negotitations for the nations of Europe to centralise "some" of the powers considered essential for an United Europe to meet the challenges of the next century. These powers have been ceded, often in bruising national referenda, by countries having some of the highest living standards and educational levels in the world. The leaders of the States that form the Union of India would be well advised not to clamour for weakening the powers vested with the central government, simply because these have been misused in the past; or for the sake of populism, or short-term gains. The remedy lies elsewhere - in fielding better people for the Parliament and by appointing the right people to man central agencies and organisations, especially the autonomous ones. In any case, with the end of one party rule the sins of the past may not be visited again on the country, atleast not to the same extent if the public, press and judiciary remain vigilant and do not allow any diminishment in their independent functioning.

The Process of Revitalisation

The provisions governing the use of article 356 have been gone into by the Sarkaria Commission which made several recommendations to check the blatant misuse of the article. It is not as if the provisions of the article were not clear. In most cases, where it was used merely to safeguard the interests of the ruling party or to quell opposition, the implied extra-constitutionality was fully comprehended by everyone. In almost every case public and press condemnation followed swiftly. That it made no difference to the rulers of the day is a separate issue. Its misuse started with the wielders of near absolute power (and lack of accountability) under the one party dispensation continued over several decades. Their opponents, when they came to power, shed their earlier inhibitions and, in turn, became equally blatant in its misuse. That is hardly surprising. It is the reason why the public tars all politicians with the same brush.

Coming to matters of immediate concern it would be universally conceded that the State of Bihar, if not already in its death throes, would soon reach that stage the way things are going. Administration, wherever it existed, is in a state of collapse. Law and order has deteriorated. Even if guilty politicians and officials are brought to book speedily there will hardly be any amelioration in the actual living conditions of the people. Terminal degeneracy has set in. No matter which lot of politicians replaces the previous lot governance is not going to improve perceptibly. It is here that the strength of the Constitution comes in. It is here where the peoples of India can "collectively" come to the rescue of their brethren in Bihar—a State where the people, under the guise of democracy, are suffering a tyranny far worse than any suffered in the turbulent centuries that preceded consolidation under British rule. Article 356 was tailor-made for the situation obtaining in Bihar today. At this point of time the "amelioration" of the unsupportable plight of the peoples of the State must take precedence over all other considerations.

President's rule should be imposed in Bihar under Article 356 without further ado with or without an all-party consensus. Should the parties demur the Government bolstered by a perception, shared by almost everyone, that the situation in Bihar has indeed deteriorated to an unacceptable degree, should order the imposition of President's rule in its own right. This time the President's rule can be a model which people would respect for all times to come. The model should remove the general fear from the minds of political parties that the ruling coalition, or any component thereof, would stand to gain from the imposition of President's rule due to any biased conduct on the part of the interim administrators. The outlines of a *Model President's Rule* are spelled out below:

A new Governor (no aspersion is intended on the present incumbent), respected by all segments of society, to be nominated along with the imposition of President's rule. The personal conduct of the Governor should harmonise with the ethos of the land. During the period of the President's rule the new Governor would function in a manner analogous to the functioning of the President of India i.e. under normal circumstances he would be bound by the advice of an Administrative Council nominated for the duration of the President's rule by the Centre.

The *Administrative Council* (hereinafter referred to simply as the Council), comprising nine members would be nominated along with the new Governor. Where the incumbent is not required to be changed the Council would still be nominated at the time of proclamation of President's Rule. This Council, whose panel would be prepared by the Home Minister, would also have to be approved by an interim committee comprising the Prime Minister, Home Minister, Speaker of the Lok Sabha and the Leader of the Opposition. The main criterion for selecting the members of the Council would be that the appointees should be persons of integrity possessing a "well-founded" reputation for impartiality, dedication and competence. The members could be from the administrative services, retired armed forces officers, technocrats, legal luminaries and the like. The private sector need not be excluded. For the duration of their tenure the members of the Council would be given all privileges and emoluments obtaining for secretaries to the Government of

India. The Council would "automatically" stand dissolved on the restoration of popular rule and their emoluments and privileges cease, within thirty days of the swearing in the new ministry.

The Governor and the Council would be required to concentrate primarily on restoration of administrative vigour and the rule of law, pending the return of elected representatives. In the process the Council would enjoy all powers vested in the Governor during the President's rule as well as additional powers specifically conferred upon it by the Centre. Concomitantly, special efforts would be directed towards restoring competence, credibility and excellence in the departments of health, education and all aspects related to poverty alleviation, women's emancipation, ecological restoration and population stabilisation. Anti-social elements would be weeded out ruthlessly during this period. The centre would provide all assistance to post competent officers of high integrity from any department or organisation during the period of revitalisation of the democratic process and restoration of good governance under President's rule. Major policy decisions, which could be construed as falling within the domain of political decision-making, would be avoided.

Only the bare outline of the Model for President's Rule uner article 356 of the Constitution, restricted to cases of terminal degeneracy with a single point programme of restoring the rule of law, has been spelled out in this article. Sensible refinements can be made at any stage. The model can be extended to other areas of administrative concern. It would be seen that the model does not visualise a radical departure from any of the constitutional provisions in vogue.

Transition

Irrespective of the present turbulence fundamental changes in the people's perception of politicians and the political process is taking place all round. Barring the really tainted variety of political leaders of the old school many politicians themselves are coming around to the point of view that "sacrificing the national interest for the sake of yesterday's power brokers" might not turn out to be a sound proposition in the long run. A few politicians have even started demanding that their party hierarchies loosen their tenacious hold on party machines. However tentative, these are welcome signs. Therefore, whilst the country deliberates upon long term political reforms several interim measures that can be implemented through an informed dialogue amongst all concerned segments are spelled out in the ensuing paragraphs.

The most important of these relates to extensions and the need to abide by service rules. In a country the size of India nobody should be indispensable, atleast not in the field of administration. Therefore extensions must not be given to anybody. Since it would be extremely difficult to enforce this rule with immediate effect it should be possible to arrive at a consensus amongst the political parties, in the Parliament, amongst the Chief Ministers and in the bureaucracy itself that with effect from 1 January 2000 no extensions would be given to any incumbent on any count. The administrative services themselves should also pass resolutions to the effect that any government servant seeking or accepting extensions would stand ostracised. An inviolable set of barriers need to be created. The Press, the Public, Chambers of Commerce and the like should also become part of the social boycott process.

It is not fully appreciated that extensions are killing excellence and leading to unhealthy and undemocratic practices. The trend is not confined to the administrative services and law and order agencies. Scientific bodies, think tanks, other government-funded bodies and public sector enterprises have all fallen prey to this disease. The armed forces have remained professional largely because the government did not allow this pernicious practice to take root in the forces. Recent attempts to make inroads must be vehemently opposed.

Organisations and bodies which have been terminally degraded cannot be easily turned around to accountability and transparent functioning. In some cases the rot is too deep. For all such terminally sick bodies the surest way to set things right would be to wipe the slate clean and start afresh. The methodology of the *tabula rasa* approach has been spelled out in "Politics in Sports" (published in *Politics India*, December, 1996). The steps enumerated therein can be applied across the board to other sectors. It is further recommended that all National Commissions (in areas not related to national security) should be given the additional mandate for presenting their reports to the Government, Parliament and other bodies to generate free discussion on their recommendations. After due deliberations by all concerned the Commission itself would be empowered to oversee the approved changes within given time frames. The Commission would, thereafter, stand dissolved after giving a final report to the Parliament.

In as far as it relates to good order and good governance - even elementary governance - serious thought has to be given to the imposition of a form of "judicial restraint" on tainted politicians and bureaucrats against whom *prima facie* cases have been established. In all such cases the concerned persons should be deemed to be "restrained" from holding any public office from the time of framing of the charge sheet till the finalisation of the case. Concomitantly, procedures can be established for the speedy disposal of such cases. Such judicial restraint would be in keeping with the highest democratic traditions.

At this juncture it would be prudent and desirable to uphold both the letter as well as the spirit of the law to safeguard the interest of the oppressed populace. And finally, overriding national priority must now be given to population stabilisation and ecological restoration. No more ground can be yielded on these counts if any semblance of democratic order is to be retained in the country. In ecologically fragile areas the cause for disquiet is so great that the full force of an enhanced TADA should be brought into immediate effect under a core group functioning directly under the Prime Minister with an independent, specially equipped, special protection group for endangered species. The mystery and mystique of India throughout the ages has related largely to its forests, flora and fauna. Destroy these and you destroy India's real heritage - and its soul.

A Ray of Hope

The people of India are awakening. Nine hundred and fifty million citizens are not going to allow a few hundred self-serving politicians and misguided civil servants to stand between them and the country's destiny any longer. Destiny still beckons. At long last, the citizens themselves have heard the clarion call. In the coming millennium India has a role to play in the comity of nations. It will contribute to the global fraternity by providing alternative models for the cultural and spiritual well-being as well as the economic betterment of mankind; not by pontificating as has been its wont in the past but by quietly demonstrating these strengths in the subcontinent as a whole. It has to indicate more harmonious (and humane) pathways to replace the destructive models in the ascendant today. Before embarking on its global mission, however, India must "first" cleanse and strengthen itself. The process is under way.

*Based on a talk delivered in 1996.

4

ELECTIONS AND THE POLITICAL CLASS

MRGG APPEAL TO THE INDIAN VOTER (1996)

For a long time voters in India have been lending their ears to appeals based on caste, creed and religion. Where has this got them and India? Has it led to an improvement of conditions in their hamlets, towns and cities? Has communal harmony improved? Has law and order improved? Are people sleeping easier? Has exploitation of the poor and downtrodden come to an end? Has corruption ceased? What became of the people's dreams of a better life for their children? Did India became stronger or did it weaken to such an extent that even smaller and less powerful nations threaten it? Where did the country lose its way? How did it end up in such a mess?

The country lost its way because it listened to the voice of unreason. It ended up in such a mess because its voters responded to the appeal of small people bent upon sowing hatred and discord. They decided to part company with the wisdom of this ancient land. They stopped heeding the real message of the great religions which flourished in this great country for centuries. Being the inheritors of one of the greatest heritages of mankind, they ended up nearly destroying that heritage. While the world has moved ahead, they continue to wallow in poverty, filth and misery. The leaders who have been voted to power on narrow caste and creed basis have ended up aggrandising themselves while pushing the country into insecurity and insolvency. Whatever the politicians might say, the ground reality is that at the end of fifty years after Independence, India is mired in the debt trap, the poverty trap and the filth trap. Is there a way out? Can something be done about it?

A clean sweep is the only way out. This means that younger, brighter and cleaner persons have to be elected in place of the existing lot of politicians who have virtually bankrupted the nation, both physically and morally.

The choice before the Indian voters is simple; do they want more of the same, or do they want India to move ahead. The decision is theirs. It is said: as you sow, so shall you reap. Voters must exercise their choice with care.

MRGG APPEAL TO THE PARLIAMENTARIANS OF THE THIRTEENTH LOK SABHA

The din of elections is behind you. You are about to enter the portals of the most hallowed institution of Indian democracy. You have now become the repositories of the aspirations of India's teeming millions, the vast majority steeped in grinding poverty. What do they expect of you?

Your foremost duty, before all else, is to apply salve on the wounds inflicted during elections. Forget the past. Look to the future.

You have been sent to the capital city to address the larger national concerns; even if you happen to be a person of the most humble origins, from an area so remote that not many people would have heard of it, in taking your seat in the national parliament you automatically become endowed with a majesty that can be diminished only by your own conduct. Be ever mindful of the fact that if you allow your stature to be diminished, by conduct unbecoming of a national parliamentarian, it is not only you who are diminished. You will thereby be diminishing, in some small measure, the self-respect of every citizen of the country. Therefore, effect simplicity and conduct yourself with decorum. Ostentation and waste are not the culture of this land. They are the culture of lands that threaten our freedom and dignity.

While you cannot turn your face from the winds of change sweeping the globe you must not be unmindful of the appalling misery in which the majority of your countrymen find themselves. In finding a mean between the pull towards greater prosperity of some segments and the drag of deprivation of others it has to be remembered that progress does not necessarily lie in bringing down the former. It lies in raising the level of the latter. The best way of achieving this is to empower the downtrodden, at the grass roots, by giving them greater opportunity. In doing so, do not drive away the talented from your shores; to seek their fortunes in other climes. It is not possible to mass produce excellence. Talent and merit, therefore, must be given their due.

You should not be unheedful of the anxiety expressed everywhere at the prospect of what was being referred to as a 'hung' parliament or shaky coalitions. Remember, the country is vast enough, amorphous enough, and resilient enough to democratically manage any change that is necessitated by the threat to its very cohesion and integrity. You are the vectors of that change. The mental association formed by the words coalition government in relation to the type of politicians that people have become used to, could have one meaning. It could have an entirely different connotation for a new set of representatives who just might have a changed concept of national security and parliamentary decorum. Many of you, not carrying any deadwood from the past, could decide to first supply a vital dose of oxygen for reviving democracy before starting to bicker about the spoils of office. Should you still get sucked into the quagmire of unprincipled politics it would be worth keeping the larger national interest in mind; in areas which for all national-minded citizens should be forever beyond petty trade-offs. If these larger concerns, relating to national security, education, women's emancipation, alleviation of poverty, environment, population stabilisation and law and order are addressed by all of you jointly, the nation need never look back.

If you are conscious of the dangers confronting your country the composition of the new Lok Sabha should give you quiet satisfaction. It could be a time for introspection; a time for renewal. The intrinsic strengths of the country are still greater than its weaknesses. The honest citizens still vastly outnumber the dishonest elements. Indian democracy has come to an historic turning point. It is for you to prove the cynics wrong. You have to show the world that the spirit of tolerance is as strong as ever in this land, home to the largest and most varied democracy in the world. The public at large, from the very humble to the very able, are sick of divisive politics. The silent majority that sent you to the Lok Sabha is ready to launch a strong and united India into the second decade of the next century. It is for you to take up the challenge and not disappoint, yet again, your long-suffering countrymen who have reposed their faith in you.

There are many things wrong with our country. It has, however, hidden strengths which are not perhaps to be found elsewhere in the world. If you have the patience you too can tap those eternal reservoirs of India's timeless wisdom. If you can learn to drink from these well-springs the riches that will be yours would be far greater than those provided by the coin of the realm. The choice is yours. Choose well.

COURT ON 'NEGATIVE VOTE'

I am writing in connection with the notice issued by the Supreme Court to the Attorney General on a petition seeking a right for the voter to cast a "negative vote" in an election by choosing the "none of the candidates" option in the electronic voting machine (EVM).

As convener Movement for Restoration of Good Government (MRGG) I have been closely involved with several issues relating to electoral reforms and have a different opinion on this matter, which I am now putting before your Lordship for consideration. I believe that the negative vote incorporation could stir a hornet's nest. My reasons are spelled out in the ensuing paragraphs.

The negative vote or 'none of the above' feature could be used by communal groups to vitiate the electoral process. For example, a religious leader in a given constituency might issue a *fatwa* for the casting of a negative vote unless candidates were put up from a particular denomination. Just one example has been given. There are others.

It is also worth considering as to how many voters possess any real knowledge about the numerous candidates whose names appear on the list when they go and exercise their vote. Even some of the well read amongst them would not have information about all the candidates, many of whose names are put up at the last moment. The time is simply not enough for the average voter to inform himself/herself about the background and potential of all the candidates.

I believe this issue has far-reaching ramifications that have not been fully explored by all concerned.

INDIAN PRESIDENTIAL ELECTION 2007– A ZERO SUM GAME

(Addressed to All Indians Who Can Feel, See, Hear and Who Care)

That the downslide in the Indian polity, which has been going on for many years, is fast reaching its nadir is borne out by the manner in which the selection of the President has been conducted by the political class and, furthermore, the style in which electioneering is being orchestrated. A quick glance first at the selection procedure.

The Selectors Cabal

- **The Ruling Party.** Not more than half-a-dozen people who call the shots, all vying with each other to show their loyalty to the dynasty; are rewarded accordingly. The present head of the dynasty having already reduced the stature of the Prime Minister to its lowest point since Independence would now like to create a similar dependency in the Rashtrapati Bhawan. *Concern for the national interest or the dignity of the highest office was never a consideration.* To quote the media, the ultimate choice, where due diligence evidently had not taken place, was the lowest common denominator in the search for consensus within the UPA.
- **The UPA (or the governing coalition):** The coalition partners were generally willing to follow the ruling Congress provided there were to be a consensus within the UPA. The major wreckers of the consensus within UPA were the Left parties led by the CPM.
- **The Left Parties:** The principal wreckers who have ceaselessly undermined government consensus on practically every major issue. Again the decision-making cabal comprised less than six people.

- **The Principal Opposition Party:** One point agenda to try and foist a person most suited to their right wing ideology. The cabal at the top comprising doddering old leaders of yesteryear who simply will not let younger people come up to revive the decline in the party. Their own fossilisation resulted in the selection of a candidate who is older than their tired selves.
- **The leader of the BSP:** Reaches agreement with the Congress leader on mutually beneficial considerations (well documented by the media). Neither leader interested in a person of eminence and integrity becoming the President.
- **The Other Political Parties** (collectively calling themselves the Third Front). A motley group; the less said about their concern for dignity, decorum or concern for the national interest the better.
- **Common to all the political parties** (mentioned above). Zero inner party democracy or consultation with the rank and file. No concern for what the people of India are saying or feel about the nationally humiliating political machinations.
- **The Present Incumbent:** Had won the respect of the nation. Was immensely popular. Could have gone out in a blaze of glory. At the end of the day slipped from the pedestal and barely remained standing. His predecessor, another respected figure who had conducted himself with dignity throughout his presidential tenure fell from grace under exactly similar circumstances.

We The People of India (The Largest Democracy in the World). Had absolutely no role to play in the selection process. The political class was and remains totally immune to the voice of the overwhelming law-abiding, non-agitating, non-rabble rousing majority. Technically, since the party cabals have taken over, the people of India, at this stage of the election, are as removed from the process of electing the president as would be an astronaut sitting on the moon watching the process without in any way being able to affect it. In other words just about thirty people (the cabalists), perhaps each one having several skeletons in his or her cupboard, and many of whom are known to have subverted and continue to subvert the legal process, decided the outcome, completely disregarding the views of one billion plus Indians. Reduced to its essentials this is the stark reality, which the people of India, the Election Commission and the Courts must face. The system worked reasonably well the way it was designed when the legislators who form the Electoral College were people of standing and when such a large percentage of them were not criminals, bootleggers, mafia dons, tax-dodgers, smugglers of people, currency, goods and the like. Evidently, something needs to be done before the next presidential election.

Media Restraint

The very manner of choosing the candidates selected by the political cabal was such that everybody was kept guessing till almost the very end. It might have been deliberate, or there might have been other reasons, including the difficulty of arriving at a consensus. Therefore, due diligence about the candidates could not be carried out - an essential exercise in any democracy for the persons likely to occupy the highest office in the country. It resulted in the media trying to dig up every bit of dirt on the candidate most likely to carry the day - in this case, as things stand, Mrs. Pratibha Patil. To tabulate the accusations, or besmirchment attempts to date by the opposition politicians and the media and other interested parties, these have been described as:

- She felt that *the time had come to remove the veil.* She quoted or misquoted or partially quoted historical texts. The result: the main proposer, the Congress Party felt embarrassed. Muslim clergy were quick to take offence. Mrs Patil tried to cover her confusion.

- Mrs Patil, while a minister in the State government was a strong votary of *population stabilisation*. She is supposed to have said that, "those who objected on grounds of religion should be ignored, because the need of the hour (according to her) was family planning, it being the highest religion (of prime importance) for India". She has been pilloried on this score as well.
- **Activities related to her Trust** that cannot stand scrutiny. They show her in very poor light.
- **She believes in spirits,** having attended the session that was run by the Brahmakumaris in Mt. Abu.

Comments of Citizens not party to media denigration, exposures or partisan politics.

- Mrs. Patil would actually be congratulated by most non-partisan Indians for having taken the lead in saying that the time has come for the women of India to be emancipated. That is the essence of her comment, even if the historical context can be questioned. The fact is that the objections have generally come from the hardliners, the Muslim clergy and opposition members. Who has bothered to take a sounding of how the veiled and oppressed women, often treated as chattel, actually feel about Mrs. Patil's statement?
- **Family Planning.** Mrs. Patil should get full marks if she made that statement and if she still holds those views. It is the prime concern for India, which most politicians have shied away from. India has one of the highest percentages of low birth weight indices in the world. Malnourished, mentally retarded children can be seen in practically every slum and *bustee* in the country. The majority of the women in the slums do not want so many children. Most of them simply keep coming, because of the nightly onslaught of the drunken male, and because family planning facilities have not reached them.

- **She believes in spirits or mediums.** What a travesty of facts. She attended a session where thousands others were present. On coming out she was confronted by the media and perhaps did not want to offend the people who invited her or did not know how her remarks would be construed. Whatever her inner feelings or beliefs, is she not entitled to them? Incidentally, the organisation that invited her at Mt. Abu is accredited to the United Nations and had been invited to set up their representation in New York. Mr. Kofi Annan, the previous Secretary General is known to have showered praise on them. Before the last general election that brought the Congress Party to power, its leader visited Mt. Abu to meet the same *dadis*. President Kalam and some of the most eminent people from around the world who have had interaction with the Brahmakumaris have been very effusive in their praise. Hardly anybody who comes into contact with the Dadis, many in the eighties, can fail to be impressed by their humaneness, childlike purity and spirituality. Their dedication has allowed the organisation to set up thousands of centres in over 90 countries. So much for mischievous media comments.
- **The way her Trust was run leaves much to be desired.** This is indeed a *very* serious allegation. If proved, should in normal circumstances *lead to her opting out of the race.*

All things being equal and seeing that practically all politicians of today (barring a handful of honourable exceptions) have many more skeletons in their cupboard and are party to illegalities of far more serious nature if investigated, or allowed to be investigated, the question that should be uppermost is, "seeing that there are only two serious contenders left in the fray, how far should the media go in continuously denigrating the lady, who all things said and done, has a very dignified bearing, and who for her entire political life has comported herself with dignity and decorum, something that is alien to most of our politicians today". Because, if the process is carried too far and in the process she is pulverised to a degree that there is no respect left for the person how will she be able to discharge her presidential duties in the years to come. It being probable that she is the candidate most likely to succeed a thought should be given to this aspect by the media. Meanwhile, the people of India have to find a way out of the political mire into which a reasonable electoral system has now been pushed. Will this become the norm or is there a way out?

KUDOS TO ELECTION COMMISSION FOR BIHAR POLLS

On behalf of MRGG I write to compliment the Election Commission for its achievement in Bihar. The Commission has worked without fear or favour. Those who do better in the elections will shower it with encomiums, while others who are worsted will pour scorn and make all sorts of wild accusations.

You should be immune to both praise and opprobrium from the political class. The public at large is highly appreciative of the remarkable work of the Commission. It could serve as a benchmark for all future elections, a veritable trendsetter. When the bricks keep flying be assured of public support across the length and breadth of India on the part of the average citizen, the proverbial common man.

We believe that Shri Rao should be awarded the Bharat Ratna for his outstanding commitment to the cause of democracy. More strength to the Election Commission's elbow.

THE SONIA FACTOR IN CONGRESS VICTORY

The swearing-in of Dr. Manmohan Singh as the new Prime Minister will mark the end of the Vajpayee era. It brings down the curtain on the high drama that followed the political upheaval brought on by the election results announced on May 13, 2004. In the post-election analyses no stone seems to have been left unturned in looking for the reasons for the decline of the Hindu right wing party on one side and the spectacular reversal of fortunes for the Congress Party, led by Sonia Gandhi on the other. In the same vein, Sonia Gandhi's motives in first inching her way forward to the prime ministership and the subsequent decision not to accept the exalted post have also been analysed in great detail by commentators in India and abroad. When the dust - perhaps not the heat generated in the electoral battle - finally settles down the parting remarks of the outgoing Prime Minister Atal Bihari Vajpayee were, in a way, prophetic when he said that while his Party had lost, Indian democracy had won. It is an apt summation of the recent elections by a statesman who has left an inimitable - and indelible - imprint on the art of running coalition governments. An equally pithy conclusion appeared in the French daily, *Le Figaro*. It captured the essence of what had taken place in India in mid-May 2004 when it said that 'within a week, India had in any case given a superb lesson in democracy to the world; a democracy whose star will remain Sonia Gandhi, 'foreigner' or not'.

Gentleman PM

While Sonia Gandhi will continue to call the shots - having ensured a vice-like grip on the party that she resurrected virtually single-handedly - attention will shift to Dr. Manmohan Singh. The former Union Finance Minister, author of the post-1991 reforms, is reputedly one of the cleanest figures in Indian politics. A man of innate humility, impeccable manners and unfailing courtesy, he will head the country's first-ever Congress coalition, christened the United Progressive Alliance (an appellation reportedly chosen by Manmohan Singh himself). Several months ago, when he could hardly have dreamed of becoming the Prime Minister - at least in not so short a while—a foreign journalist asked him as to what he considered to be the most important issue before India. Manmohan Singh had no hesitation in replying, 'the mass poverty of India'.

Core Issue

And herein lies the rub. The Bharatiya Janata Party (BJP) lost the elections because – as per many - it had not paid sufficient attention to the needs of rural India. The incoming dispensation is bound to get its priorities right in this regard, more so since it is dependent upon the left parties for its stability in Parliament. Although the new government might be able to make an initial dent, it will soon hit its head against a hard reality. Hardly any government at the Centre is likely to be in a position to make a meaningful reduction in rural poverty unless it seriously tackles the issue of population proliferation. With 20 million more mouths to feed every year and 9 million fresh entrants into the job market where is the question of being able to usher in poverty reduction for the masses in India or, for that matter, the subcontinent, no matter how sound the government policies. To cite an example, easily comprehensible by lay persons of the horrendous nature of the runaway population growth on the subcontinent, suffice it to say that even if ten thousand persons could be transported to new colonies in far away lands every day of the year, it would not make a significant dent in the growing population mass - most of it low birth weight, begotten by misery-stricken people, living in sub human conditions.

There are many other reasons for good policies generally falling by the wayside in the countries of the subcontinent. In India, the sorry state of administration in states like Bihar is a case in point. The Bihar model of governance has become a byword for governance degeneration. Uttar Pradesh and a few other states could also go the Bihar way, if they are not careful. What is true of India applies equally to Pakistan and Bangladesh. Rural poverty and the general decline across the length and breadth of the subcontinent, except in a few isolated pockets, will remain the order of the day unless the governments of these countries give overriding priority to population stabilisation, albeit in a non-coercive manner.

Populism Vs Poverty

Compulsion of the Chinese variety need not come into it for the simple reason that failure to stabilise population is more on account of organisational infirmity than the many other reasons generally cited. It is estimated that today up to fifty per cent or so of births taking place are the result of unwanted pregnancies. Evidently, meaningful population stabilisation may not be achievable at this stage without concomitant emphasis on women's emancipation and much higher outlays on health, hygiene and education. Higher allocations by themselves, were they to be made in future due to altered priorities, will still not yield the desired results because the administrative instrumentalities of the governments of the subcontinent for implementing these decisions at the business end have been blunted and corrupted to a degree that makes them practically useless as harbingers of change in the positive direction. To compound the problem, many governments, immediately on assuming office or just before elections, resort to unabashedly populist measures that can never be a panacea for poverty reduction. Yet state after state goes in for such populism in spite of fiscal deficits running into double digits.

By the same token, it would be unfair to solely blame the outgoing BJP government for the ills that afflict rural India in UP, Bihar and several other states. In quite a few of these states BJP governments were not in power. Massive central allocations for programmes that could have made a difference, or should have made a difference, were frittered away - the famous fodder scam in Bihar is just one example - by the regional satraps who destroyed the strong foundations of law and order and administration that obtained in these states during the British rule and in the early decades following independence. Latent governance stability existed in most of the states of the Hindi heartland till well into the 1970s. Emergency and the Sanjay Gandhi induced dispensations put paid to good governance. In Pakistan, and subsequently in Bangladesh, the rot had started much earlier. It has gotten institutionalized to a far greater degree than in India. India is fortunate in its diversity, plurality, the strength of institutions like the higher Judiciary, Election Commission and, as demonstrated in the recent elections, the rock-solid deepening of democracy. What continues to astound observers from around the world and Indians themselves is the remarkable perceptiveness of the average Indian voter, who with unfailing regularity continues to give the boot - both at the Centre and the States- to governments that fail to perform or to leaders who become too powerful and arrogant. Elections in India are the great levelers. During elections 2004, Indian voters have put all political parties on notice, perform or bite the dust. This remarkable feature of Indian democracy will now have a spillover effect in many other countries of the subcontinent, especially Pakistan. The yearning for true democracy, Indian style, could become irresistible for the people of Pakistan and many other countries that watched the Indian exercise with amazement, exhilaration and a touch of envy. Like the Bollywood films the pull of Indian democracy could prove irresistible. It could sound the death knell for authoritarian regimes on India's periphery. The change could come sooner than expected.

FOREIGN ORIGIN: THE NATIONAL SECURITY ANGLE

Hon'ble Chief Justice

In a news item, in the *Times of India,* New Delhi, dated April 17, 2007 the opposition party, which had held Sonia Gandhi's foreign origin as an issue against her taking on any constitutional office asked the Congress party to initiate a political debate over the matter. The opposition party's call for a debate followed the admission of a petition by the Supreme Court on whether a person of foreign origin could hold a constitutional office. Although the Supreme Court had earlier, on an election petition, ruled that Sonia Gandhi was an Indian citizen, the petitioner, however, got around the ruling by so framing the petition as to focus on her competence to hold an office at the highest level in the country.

The controversy regarding Ms. Sonia Gandhi has unnecessarily taken on a political hue and the clamour against her a political bias. In the political cacophony thus generated the true import of the question of denial of the highest office to a citizen of foreign origin and, more importantly, with thriving foreign familial and business connections is lost site of. Very simply stated the nation cannot afford to take a chance. It has nothing to do with the persona of Ms. Sonia Gandhi. It has everything to do with national security and the supreme national interest. Today NATO forces are deployed in Afghanistan, not too far from the borders of India. They are already making forays into NWFP and FATA of Pakistan. Should the situation deteriorate further they might make deeper inroads into Pakistan, thereby coming much closer to the Indian border. Currently, India's relations with the West are on a reasonably good footing owing to the common perception of threat from global terrorism. It should be recalled, nevertheless, that not too far back the West was siding with Pakistan and even China-Italy included. Even today several western countries, again including Italy, are opposed to India's nuclear stand. Hypothetically, as Prime Minister, Ms. Sonia Gandhi being a person of foreign origin from a NATO country would be the final arbiter of several decisions regarding India's security. Should India ever have to confront NATO she would almost certainly face mental anguish, torn between conflicting loyalties to her natural motherland and her adopted land. It is not inconceivable that India might have to retaliate against NATO forces including Italian forces should India perceive a danger to itself. Under these circumstances the question should *never* arise of a foreign origin person being the ultimate arbiter of India's security. An example has been given of only the National Security aspect. Similar examples can be given from other fields where clash of interest between India and Europe could take place in the coming years.

It is felt that the argument put forward against foreign origin persons holding the highest office in the land, or, for that matter, any office that has a bearing on national security is unassailable. Your Lordships might like to take note before giving a definitive ruling on the subject.

5

JUDICIARY: THE SAVING GRACE

TAKING THE PIL ROUTE

The decline in the quality of governance linked to the criminalisation of politics and the degeneration of the law and order machinery in the country has been forcing the public to seek redress before the courts. Where the inability of the government - regardless of its cause - to take suitable measures to safeguard the public interest affects large segments of the public or the interest of future generations, Public Interest Litigation (PIL) has remained one of the few avenues available to stem the rot or to set things right. A number of instances can be cited were the lack of concern on the part of the government or its functionaries could have led to incalculable harm to public health, public interest or the ecological future of the country. In very many cases government apathy was seen to have resulted from vote bank politics, indifference, improper analyses, criminalisation of politics, or undue pressure from vested interests. Because the intervention of the courts often *did* lead to redress, the public has increasingly felt that the PIL route represents the surest and perhaps the *sole* option available to it to set things right.

In the light of the foregoing, the number of PILs that have come before the courts have shown considerable increase. Should the degenerative processes in government continue it is possible that the number of PILs that come before the courts rise exponentially. Added to the backlog of cases already before the courts an enormous increase in the number of PILs may tend to swamp their functioning. It has also to be remembered that at any given time the number of frivolous PILs that come before the courts will also show increase. Therefore, there is need to bring in a semblance of order and functional streamlining into a process that due to its very efficacy might become unwieldy or inordinately time consuming.

To ensure that the remedy available to non-governmental organisations and individuals seriously dedicating their lives to social upliftment, preservation of the environment, restoration of good governance and similar activities, which collectively add to national betterment through PILs is not diluted due to frivolous petitioning or runaway increase in numbers, a method has to be found to retain the efficacy of this recourse available to the public, without letting it get snowed under due to the unmanageable increase (in numbers). Against this background the via media approach placed for consideration of their Lordships comprises the following basic steps:

All PILs received by the highest court in the land or any of the High Courts would be graded according to importance and urgency by a designated quasi-judicial body consisting of retired justices of the Supreme Court or High Courts and eminent lawyers / scientists / media persons or any other eminent person considered suitable by the nominating body. The body that could be designated as the 'PIL Scrutiny Committee' (PSC) will grade the PILs into four categories. The first category, termed category A PILs, will include PILs that in the opinion of the PSC should be accorded the highest priority for consideration by the courts due to the overriding importance of the PIL in the national interest, interest of the public at large, or for the interest of future generations. The second category, or category B PILs would be those PILs which are considered admissible on a lower priority i.e. delay in their consideration would not harm the national interest, the interest of the public at large, the interest of the coming generations, grave injustice being perpetrated or for any other reason. The third category, or category C PILs would be those that merit consideration, but which can be dealt with through alternative pathways (that have been spelt out later on in the paper). The fourth category or category D PILs would be those PILs, which can be dismissed straightaway by the designated body as being frivolous or not of sufficient merit. Their consideration would unnecessarily swamp the judicial process.

The quasi-judicial body (PSC) for classification of PILs would be a five-member body, which can be set up in all states having a separate High Court. The panel of names could be chosen *suo motu* by a serving justice of the Supreme Court, the Chief Justice of the High Court concerned and the Law Secretary of the state in which the High Court is located. The bodies thus constituted could be nominated for a single tenure of five years each. For rejection of a PIL it would have to be approved by at least three of the five members on grounds of it being frivolous or lacking in merit. To ensure smooth functioning of the PSC back up or standby members could also be chosen at the time of the initial selection so that work is not held up due to illness or non-availability of a member.

As mentioned earlier, category 3 or category C PILs would be considered for alternative method of being dealt with. The alternative pathway reduced to its essentials means that the PSC arrives at the opinion that the PIL prima facie has considerable merit and could - all things being equal - meet with favourable outcome if the judicial process is gone through. In all such cases, the merit of the PIL would be the determining criterion. To save time and legislative costs to all concerned, the PSC would express an opinion for consideration of the government department or the official concerned to the effect that since an examination of the PIL has revealed a high probability of the prayer being granted it would be advisable for the government department or the official body concerned to take remedial measures within a suitable time frame. If the opinion of the PSC is accepted by the government department concerned the latter would intimate its acceptance as well as the remedial measures that would be taken by the department as also the time frame in which these would be implemented. Should, however, the government department not wish to abide by the opinion of the PSC it would have to intimate their decision of non-compliance within 90 days. In the latter case, i.e., non-compliance with the opinion of the PSC, the government department would have to bear the costs of the litigation and all reasonable expenses undertaken by the petitioner filing the PIL in the public interest.

The methodology outlined above provides a framework for streamlining the process of PIL consideration by the judiciary. It also aims to reduce the burden on the judiciary keeping in mind the time factor involved. More importantly, it puts officialdom on notice that where all reasonable indicators reveal that a PIL has merit, is in the public interest, and has high probability of being looked at favourably by the judiciary the government should streamline its own functioning in a manner that officials do not act as barriers to natural advancement and public well-being merely on account of bureaucratic inertia, obduracy or sheer cussedness. Concomitantly, the public would also be made aware that there is a need to avoid frivolous or ill-considered petitioning of the courts. The recommendations made above serve as a starting point for streamlining the PIL process. Modifications and improvements can be made from time to time by all concerned from reception to adoption to institutionalization.

INELUCTABLE NEED FOR THE CHIEF ELECTION COMMISSIONER, ELECTION COMMISSIONERS AND CAG TO BE SELECTED BY A COLLEGIUM

[MRGG missive to the incoming Chief Justice of the Supreme Court]

It hardly needs reiteration that each passing year the bona fides of the government are becoming more and more suspect in the eyes of public. This is one of the main reasons for the increase in PILs relating to governance issues and corruption at the highest levels. The recent cases relating to black money and major scams before the Supreme Court, including the appointment of the CVC, are clearly indicative of mala fide actions on the part of the government. Dissimulation and prevarication, including before the highest judicial body, have also been imputed to the government in a number of cases.

In the light of the foregoing and to prevent future body blows to democracy on the part of the Executive, presently more interested in protecting party interest and party functionaries rather than the national interest and national security, the time may have come to look ahead and take appropriate *anticipatory* steps to prevent further erosion to democracy in the country.

With this background it is submitted before the Honorable Court that a Bench be nominated to decide whether the present practice of the CEC, Election Commissioners and the CAG being decided by the government of the day without a collegium could conceivably lead to partisan leanings in the selection. In the prevailing conditions a partisan approach to the appointments, to the detriment of democratic functioning, has become a very distinct possibility in civil society perception. Therefore, the Bench going into the matter might direct - or even suggest - to the government to set up credible collegiums for all future selections for the Chief Election Commissioner as also the Election Commissioners and the Comptroller and Auditor General (CAG). It becomes imperative that such collegiums be set up at the earliest based on Supreme Court direction or guidelines as in the case of CVC. It is relevant to recall here that the Supreme Court had been approached by the government in the matter several years ago when the single election commissioner was made into a three-member body on the *directions* of the Supreme Court during the tenure of the then election commissioner, Mr. T.N. Seshan. Therefore a precedent stands established.

This letter could be taken note of as a petition or PIL, as decided by your Lordship. It has the support of other NGOs including Common Cause, NNFI and Associates and several other civil society bodies. If required, their written consent to the PIL/petition could be forwarded. In either case, the issue being taken up is much too vital for the future of democracy to be left undecided till a later date, when the crisis is actually upon the country.

I have read with interest your views on PILs. As a matter of fact, I had sent a paper to an earlier Chief Justice on this very subject, recommending a system that sifted the chaff from the grain. It was published in *South Asia Politics.* Here, I would like to take this opportunity to invite your attention to the Occasional Paper No. 9 published by India International Centre based on my talk on ***"Reconciling Coalition Dharma, Good Governance and National Security".***

Along with my fellow countrymen who are saddened by the decline in the probity of our elected representatives, I wish you success – which means success for the country as well – in your endeavours to arrest the palpable decline that has set in, in most spheres of governance, both at the Centre and the States. All well-wishers of India pray for your success in what has now become the Herculean task of cleaning the Augean Stables of the governance cesspool.

NEED TO REVISIT ANTI-TERROR LAWS

(Talk delivered at the India International Centre on August 22, 2009)

Throughout recorded history, except for a brief interlude in the 20th century, the only law that prevailed during conflicts - internal or external- was the law of the jungle. It brought into the lexicon the well-used aphorism "might is right". Conflict has always been nasty and brutish, though not always short. The law of Nature, or pure Darwinism: "nature red in tooth and claw". It is only towards the close of the 19th century, when live reporting on war and the photographs related to the suffering were brought home to the drawing rooms of London and Paris, capitals of the two world powers of the time that a thought was given to the plight of the civilians caught in the turmoil and soldiers during captivity. Before that, the motto that was generally followed was "no quarter expected or given". The history of the last few thousand years is replete with tales of sacking of cities, laying waste of the countryside, rapine and plunder and, added to that, the slaughter of hundreds of thousands of unarmed civilians. It must be clearly understood that in the first half of the 20th Century before the colonial masters were deprived of their colonies, those humanitarian norms were meant primarily for the European or white people. The European nations seldom cared to apply them to the natives of the subject nations in Asia. It is only later after the telegraph connected the world more closely and England and France brought in soldiers from their colonies to fight in European wars — mainly against the Germans - that the humanitarian protocols were extended globally.

The changing nature of war, more so after 9/11, has put paid, *in practice,* to the *humanitarian conventions* on which country-specific legislations are based. The humanitarian considerations have generally been allowed to fall by the wayside when framing laws internally in practically all the countries afflicted by terrorism. India remains the exception. The reason for other countries having legislated far more draconian laws is not because the western democracies have turned their back on humanitarian concerns or that their press and civil society have not been vociferous in their opposition to the most draconian features. The reason is that all these states – almost without exception - put greater value on the lives of their *own* countrymen; a prime sovereign responsibility of any government. They understand that the security agencies that have to bear the brunt of the fight against terror to protect the state and its citizens must not be so disadvantaged by humanitarian concerns as to render them ineffective. The result of this fundamental difference in perception is there for everyone to see. The US and the western democracies have been able to considerably curb (as in the case of the US) or drastically reduce the potential of the perpetrators of terror after it became a global phenomenon after 9/11. In the case of India the less said the better. The blame for this sorry state of affairs rests directly with the political class - with their perpetual goal scoring against each other at the cost of the security of the nation. The judiciary too must take a portion of the blame. Undoubtedly every now and then grave wrongs are committed in bringing the terrorists and their supporters to book. However, seeing the scale of the operations in a country the size of India, added to its diversity these transgressions represent a percentage that is miniscule. An example will suffice. Take the case of rapes attributed to the Indian Army. If the total number of cases are taken in any calendar year in a force that numbers well over a million, and from that number are deducted the proven false allegations, often orchestrated by organisations supporting the insurgents or terrorists, it would be found that they are much below the number of rapes committed in the capital city of India in one month, which has the highest density of law and order forces. What is more where rape is proven the army acts speedily to bring the perpetrators of the rape to justice. Were onc to go by the media hype and the propaganda drummed up by interested parties the world is led to believe that the Indian Army is lax in preventing rapes.

The media in India, instead of pointing out the one-sidedness of Amnesty and other such Western organizations hell-bent on India-bashing and more purposefully Indian Army-bashing, faithfully reproduces these condemnations far and wide, providing wider internal dissemination than warranted by the mostly ill-founded or one-sided investigations.

Reducing the Dilemma to its Essentials

Simply put the dilemma in enacting laws dealing with terrorism is essentially the need of providing overriding security to the citizens of a state while ensuring that human rights are not thereby violated. This is a dilemma that will keep taxing the minds of jurists, human rights activists, human rights commissions and the states themselves. To put it plainly these exercises in jurisprudence for safeguarding the fundamental freedoms are essentially limited to practising democracies. Much the larger number of nations still function under totalitarian regimes maintaining a facade of democracy. In all such cases where there is neither the true freedom of the ballot nor of the press or the judiciary the concept of human rights and natural justice do not even enter into consideration in any meaningful way. A few of these non-democratic states, take China for example, have been able to keep a lid on internal unrest by giving the go by to the concept of basic freedoms of the individual and through the exercise of extreme state violence. Of course, no terrorism has taken place in Tibet. In the case of minorities the problem in the long-term has been settled by the expedience of demographic swamping as has happened in Tibet and Xinjiang. The dilemma is compounded for India by the fact that the country which has been exposed for the longest period of time to the scourge of terrorism has the least severe laws when compared to other practising democracies like the USA and west European countries, including UK, France and Germany.

A news item in one of the dailies had expressed the frustration rather pithily: "The Key is the confidence with which a society goes after those who assault it: today, as we have noted (above), we cannot investigate cells, we cannot pursue suspects: the hand of security forces are tied in encounters; we can't stem Bangladeshi infiltrators; we are not able to hang Afzal Guru even after the Supreme Court has confirmed the death sentence for attacking Parliament. The nature of discourse is such that the State apparatus is perpetually on the defensive". (Unquote).

The press in the western countries while clamouring for greater respect for human rights is conscious of the difficulties faced by the security agencies in trying to keep the country protected from terrorist outrages. The excerpt is from a UK newspaper: "Equally, however, let us not soar so high above the lethal ground upon which our intelligence agencies have to operate that we make their work impossible. It may satisfy some to watch the spooks squirm. But be careful what you wish for. A naticn which turns moodily on those responsible for its security is actually practising nothing more sophisticated than self-harm."

How other Countries Deal with Adversaries

"I am strongly in favour of using poisoned gas against uncivilized tribes. The moral effect should be good... and it would spread a lively terror..." (Winston Churchill commenting on the British use of poison gas against the Iraqis after the First World War).

From the statement just read out, attention is invited to the words *'the moral effect should be good* and *it would spread a lively terror'*. The words, uttered in the halcyon days of the Empire, as the British ventured into Mesopotamia after the defeat of Turkey in the First World War, provide a glimpse into the mind of the great English statesman, whose sentiment expressed over 80 years ago has apparently lingered. As envisioned by Churchill, the use of deadly, inhuman weapons–in the present case depleted uranium (DU)–did spread lively terror in Iraq–even if the rest of the world failed to see the 'moral effect.'

American pilots bombing and strafing, with depleted uranium weapons helpless retreating Iraqi soldiers, who had already surrendered, exclaimed:

"We toasted him.... we hit the jackpot....a turkey shoot....shooting fish in a barrel....basically just sitting ducks... There's just nothing like it. It's the biggest Fourth of July show you've ever seen, and to see those tanks just 'boom', and more stuff just keeps spewing out of them... they just become white hot. It's wonderful." (*L A Times* and *Washington Post*, February 27, 1991). In the invasion of Iraq in 2003, the US dropped 15,000 PGM, 7500 unguided bombs and aimed 750 cruise missiles at Iraq in about 21 days, plus a colossal amount of artillery, tanks and attack helicopter fire, not to mention mortars and small arms fire.

US policies are being increasingly condemned in practically every forum around the world that is not linked in some way to the present US administration, including all those who stand behind the US administration and benefit from its policies. There is hardly any global conference where denunciation of US policies does not take up much of the speaking and discussion time. Such universal opprobrium, which would have made most countries wince, does not seem to have made the slightest difference to the make-up of people at the helm of affairs in Washington. If anything, their resolve seems to have strengthened; the only change has been a change in tactics. For the US government the *overriding concern* is the protection of their citizenry from further acts of terror. To that extent it has to be conceded that whatever the encroachment on civil liberties the US administrations have successfully ensured that not a single act of terror has taken place on their soil after 9/11/2001, in spite of the fact that the USA remains the most targeted nation for the jihadist forces worldwide.

Across the border, Canadian Defence Chief General Rick Hillier was said to have declared of the Canadian Forces, "We are not the Public Service of Canada, we are not just another department, we are the Canadian Forces and our job is to be able to kill people." This is a complete turnabout in military doctrine from the days when Canadian forces were sent abroad ostensibly to *prevent* the killing of people.

The war on terror is leading to market forces now dominating the military scene, blurring the distinction between private and public armies, even countries, as in Iraq and Afghanistan. Wherever there is a shortfall in regular soldiers, private security agencies have been filling the gap. Nevertheless, they may still fall short of expectations when confronting stateless shadowy persons. Not being able to pin down the enemy or seize the initiative from the adversary results in more savage bombing and destruction of the infrastructure.

The shadowy aspects of warfare have taken a frightening dimension. According to a very senior Indian diplomat, the CIA publicly acknowledged, for a Canadian television documentary, that they trained the Khalistani bombers, who planted the bombs on Kanishka and the second Air India flight to India at the request of Pakistan's ISI. The training was provided at an official CIA facility in the US itself. When challeged on its morality, they retorted: "some people's terrorists are other people's freedom fighters". The documentary film was never actually shown but the Government of India reportedly managed to acquire a copy. The Canadians had steadfastly declined to co-operate with India on the arrest of the mass murderers, presumably at the behest of the CIA, until 9/11.

Until that moment, they constantly raised technical objections, refusing to accept wiretaps on the grounds that they required prior judicial authorisation. There are many who wonder whether the US clandestine agencies do not still support some Pakistani actions, including terror, murder and rape.

On January 25, 2002, White House Counsel Alberto Gonzales, who is now America's Attorney General, sent a Memorandum to President Bush in which he wrote, "The nature of the new war places a high premium on other factors, such as the ability to quickly obtain information from captured terrorists and their sponsors in order to avoid further atrocities against American civilians."

"The way the United States fights is a little different from other people. We have this document called the Constitution, and it governs everything we do in the United States - including the way the military fights". (Maj. Gen. Thomas Fiscus, Judge Advocate General of the US Air Force in an interview with the electronic edition of *Stars and Stripes*).

Whereas Muslim states all over almost *never* hesitate to enter mosques to shoot terrorists hiding inside, be it Saudi Arabia, Pakistan or other countries, in India the security forces are obliged to get their own men killed so that the Courts do not pass strictures on them. In fact, such is the extreme nature of what appears to be the bias of the courts that several years ago in Kashmir when the security forces had surrounded a mosque where insurgents were holed up the court directed that food be carried in for them. The human rights of security forces in India are invariably sacrificed at the altar of 'appearing to be more fair than any other nation in the world'. The result is that known terrorists are routinely released for want of insufficient evidence. The caption on the front page of *The Indian Express* datelined New Delhi August 21, 2009 confirms the super fairness syndrome. The caption reads "Two years in prison, top Hizbul man walks free, red faces in J&K". The point is that the courts have to take note that in recapturing the individual several more personnel of the security forces may have to lay down their lives. Even the political leaders seem to be oblivious of the need to protect the lives of *Indian* soldiers. In Assam the ULFA was twice brought to the verge of extinction in 'Operation Bajrang and Operation Rhino'.

On both occasions the Indian Army was prevented from delivering the *coup de grace* so that politicians could get into the act of showing to the world their magnanimity and statesmanship.

Dealing with Terrorism

Disproportionality Factor

(The thesis on the "Disproportionality Factor" was first unveiled a few years ago at a keynote presentation at the Technical University of Eindhoven in The Netherlands. It was published and circulated by the university.)

In taped interviews to an Afghan interrogator, two Afghans and three Pakistanis who were among 21 people arrested earlier in 2006 described their roles in the attacks, which killed at least 70 people, most of them Afghan civilians but also international peacekeepers, a Canadian diplomat and a dozen Afghan police officers and soldiers. In the tape, the men described a fairly low-budget network that begins with the recruitment of young bombers in the sprawling Pakistani port city of Karachi. The bombers are moved to safe houses in the border towns of Quetta and Chaman, and then transferred into Afghanistan, where they are provided with cars and explosives and sent out to find a target. (*HT World*, February 16, 2006 *The New York Times* Pak Blind Eye to Afghan bombings).

Disproportionality works against the forces tackling terrorism, especially terrorism of the type taken up by radical

Islamists in several countries. By now most people are fairly well acquainted with the terror breeding facilities that were set up in Pakistan and Afghanistan right up to the allied invasion of Afghanistan, following the 11/9/2001 attacks on the USA. While the Jihad factories might have collapsed in Afghanistan after the fall of Kabul in October 2001, there was hardly any let up in selected areas of Pakistan, which continue to churn out fanatical, zombie-like students in large numbers in their madrassas. The numbers of potential Jihadis can now be reckoned, in the hundreds of thousands, if not in the millions, because these institutions have since spread to many other parts of the subcontinent and beyond.

The streamlined production facilities for churning out young, radicalized, possibly misanthropic students in large numbers is not a costly exercise seeing the ready availability of young recruits from families, which although impoverished, produce children in large numbers. The average size of such families being six or seven, they are ever ready to send one, two or more children to the madrassas where they are clothed, fed and taught elementary counting besides writing in Urdu and Arabic in order to learn the Quran by rote. Not all of the products coming out of these madrassas would make high caliber terrorists. After very strict weeding out even if two or three were to be found fit for undertaking the type of terrorist strikes, including suicide missions that the world has come to dread the final count would still be impressive. With variations for time, place, or the country where Jihad factories are located the cost of training one potential terrorist is not likely to exceed forty thousand rupees, especially in the poorer districts of Pakistan. This works out to less than US $ 1000 per recruit at the production site. Thereafter, translocation to other countries and proper kitting out for the task could add to the cost by several hundred or even a few thousand dollars. Except for very exceptional cases the total cost would not exceed US $5000.

Taking the case now of the countries that are involved in the battle *against* global terrorism it will be seen that as compared to the training of an average Jihadi for carrying out terrorism acts the cost of training the average soldier involved in combating this menace would be far higher. In the case of the armies of most of the countries in Asia, for example India, The Philippines or Indonesia it could be a factor of 10 or 20. That is to say that if the cost of training an average Jihadi for undertaking terror missions works out to $5000, the cost of training an average combatant in the countries mentioned could work out to between 50,000 to 100,000 US dollars. In the case of the USA and some of the western democracies, however, the cost increase could be a factor between 50 and 100, especially when training of Special Forces is taken into account. These cost differentials continue even for persons rendered *hors de combat.* To elaborate, an injured Jihadi would be taken clandestinely to some sympathetic medical practitioner and operated upon in the most rudimentary fashion. In case of death the burial costs would be minimal. Terminal benefits to the family of the deceased would be a few hundred thousand rupees, equivalent to $4000 approximately. For impoverished families in Pakistan, that offer up their children for such activities even half that amount would be considered a windfall.

Match this amount of approximately $4,000 in case of injury or death for the Jihadi with the cost that would be incurred for a US soldier who becomes a casualty. For serious injuries the cost of evacuation (normally by helicopter) to an advance field hospital and subsequently to a facility in Europe or USA, plus the cost of treatment would work out to a differential factor upward of 1,000. For serious injuries or death the pensionary and terminal benefits would be an order of magnitude higher than those in the case of an injured or dying Jihadi.

The next item to be considered in this category is the cost of maintaining a Jihadi in the field as compared to a US or western soldier. Taking the Afghanistan theatre the cost of maintaining a Jihadi in the field for one year would seldom go beyond $1000, whereas the cost of maintaining a western soldier for the same period would go up by a factor of about 100 or so depending upon the location of the soldier or his unit. Here again, Special Forces come into a separate category.

So far the comparisons worked out related only to the training and deployment of the adversaries. We now have to consider the cost differential relating to combat scenarios.

Combat Scenarios

We move next to the cost evaluation disparities in 'live' engagements between terrorist teams and the US or NATO forces combating them. The disparity resulting from suicide missions will be taken separately at the end. Sporadic engagements between Jihadi type elements and the US forces and allies are taking place practically every day in Afghanistan. A typical incident could take any of the following forms: an IED being set off along a route where the US or International Security Assistance Force (ISAF) teams have to pass; a mortar attack at an installation or small-sized post; ambush; or hit and run operations launched from terrain that would be difficult to negotiate by foreign forces. The difficulty in terrain negotiation in mountainous country stems both from lack of the type of familiarity that local inhabitants have as also from the type of equipment used by foreign forces. In a typical ambush or hit and run operation a handful of Jihadis fire a few rockets and mortar rounds on a US convoy or position. The latter could be a temporary halting place or post occupied by a platoon-sized force. The initiative almost invariably being with the attacker (the regrouped Taliban) the opening shots in the form of various types of Small Arms (SA) would be fired from well-selected positions on the mountainside overlooking the convoy or the post. By now the retaliation procedure having also been perfected to a fine art by the US forces, the retaliation is swift. There is immediate fire in very heavy volumes by the post or the convoy attacked with integral weapons. Simultaneously the call goes out for armed helicopters and aircraft strikes. Without going into further details, tabulation can be made of the cost of the exchange to the two sides. In the case of the attackers, surprise being with the attackers, few, if any–casualties would be suffered by them, because after letting off their initial volleys the Taliban escape to a more sheltered position or simply melt away. The cost of the attack on US forces to the Taliban would not normally exceed $100. It must be noted here that there is no dearth of arms and ammunition of all types in Afghanistan. Weapons and munitions had been dumped or sent in by the Russians, Americans, Iranians and the Pakistanis in huge quantities over the years. Even now the pipeline in manpower and war-materiel from Pakistan is intact, Pakistan's frontline status in the war on terrorism notwithstanding. The cost of response to even the most elementary form of attack by a handful of Taliban fighters on a US convoy or post could exceed several million dollars.

The retaliatory US exchange would normally include the following: thousands of rounds of automatic fire, dozens of rounds of rocket and mortar fire, several rounds of tank fire, hundreds of rounds of artillery fire, plus munitions and missiles unleashed from the attack helicopters, and bombs and munitions dropped by aircraft. To this not inconsiderable fire power of all types that would have been expended has to be added the fuel cost for the helicopters and aircraft called in for close support. Even without taking into consideration personnel or vehicle casualties that may have resulted in the US force - generally caught off guard, the initiative being with the enemy - the cost disparity might work out to about one is to one or several million. It could become much higher should some persons become casualties or if a tank or helicopter were to be destroyed.

Suicide missions belong to a separate category for several reasons. To begin with retaliatory fire is neither possible in most cases nor would it be required because the target self-destructs along with whatever other carnage that might have taken place by way of the number of people killed or wounded and the other damage resulting from the detonations caused by the suicide bomber.

The analysis given above clearly brings out that over a period of time the elements indulging in terror attacks against US and Western forces and more recently against Indian forces (especially 26/11) are able to extract phenomenal costs from their adversaries, which purely in US dollar terms result in adverse ratios of one is to several million and often tens of millions. Of late the number of incidents, which were already high in Iraq, increased in Afghanistan and India as well. Besides manpower losses which the Western democracies can ill-afford, and their opponents afford ad infinitum, the financial bleeding that takes place is something that the US and its allies and India can ignore only at their peril. It does not mean that technological superiority is given the go by. It indicates, however, a change in military as well as geopolitical strategy. At the operational level it requires a radical re-think in local level initiatives and the tactics adopted by US forces and their allies in the field in Afghanistan. The same is applicable to India.

It should not be forgotten that every time an allied soldier is killed the chances are that he or she would have been the only child of its parents or one of two siblings. In the case of the Taliban fighter who is killed, he is most likely to be one of several children, possibly one out of 6, 7, 8 or even 10 or 12. Something similar is happening with the Indian Army.

Increasingly the officers killed in fighting the intruders are the only child or one of two siblings. Increasingly the soldiers in the Indian Army come from small-sized nuclear families. It is an aspect that is generally lost sight of: the heightened emotional devastation of families of US and NATO forces back home whose wards are killed in Afghanistan.

In examining disproportionality ratios between the dispensers of global terror and the forces deployed to counter them worldwide, added security costs that have gone up considerably in several domains have to be factored. These relate to heightened surveillance at airports, railways and bus termini, ports and dockyards, nuclear plants, vital bridges and installations, water supplies and so many other areas of enhanced vulnerability for civilian populations. Around the world, increased security has been provided to persons considered vulnerable to targeting by terrorists or their agents. Many businesses have seen their expenses go up considerably due to increased insurance costs. The case of airlines and shipping lines has been well documented. If all the costs that have gone up due to terror strikes, especially after 9/11 and 26/11 are taken together the total cost worldwide could conceivably run into tens of billions of dollars, possibly exceeding hundred billion dollars annually. It has also to be noted that these are recurring costs that are likely to continue till well into the future. Putting it all together the adverse ratios that were already very high for governments and security forces dealing with terrorists go up by several orders of magnitude, if the entire spectrum of enhanced global security is taken into account. Terrorists win on two counts: massive damage to civilians and property by the acts of terror plus the disproportionality alluded to in the earlier paragraphs.

Breaking the Definitional Impasse

Inhumanity will henceforth become the order of the day.

The advent of the machine on one hand and fanaticized *jehadi*-type terrorists on the other, have made it possible to evade reciprocity and responsibility. Collateral damage is being increasingly accepted as a consequence. A feature that is becoming common to both terrorism and counter terrorism is increased violence. Violence in the new wave terrorism, and its riposte in the form of counter terrorism, is marked by the recourse to methods that enhance the lethality of the vectors to increase casualties. The violence inflicted upon unsuspecting people by terrorists may appear to be random in nature – as the throwing of a grenade in a market place. It is, however, precise to the extent that the terrorist is able to decide on where and when to cause the explosion for maximum effect. Precision is, in fact, the hallmark of the most sophisticated terrorist operations. The targeting of the World Trade Centre and the Pentagon are testimony to it. The precision of the attack based entirely on human aptitude, devoid of any precision guided munitions, was no less sophisticated than the super precision aids available to the most technically advanced nation in the world. The US retaliation in Afghanistan was also based on precision targeting, notwithstanding the collateral damage in the initial phase of retaliation. Therefore, if precision is to become the hallmark, including when the terrorists choose the precision mode of attack, it could have an important bearing on the fight against terrorism in the years ahead.

People around the world were horrified at the collateral damage that took place in the wake of the American intervention in Afghanistan; and which continues to take place each time the Israeli punitive thrusts are launched into Gaza and the West Bank. Regardless of the concern expressed around the world by ordinary people not directly involved in the conflict the fact remains that heavy collateral damage will hereafter become the norm in dealing with shadowy organisations that send forth suicide bombers to cause terror and mayhem amongst innocent civilians. Their very anonymity and ability to merge back into the crowd from which they emerge to visit death and destruction on the targeted communities makes it inevitable that whatever the form of retaliation collateral damage becomes an operative condition when dealing with organisations that train people for such operations. It is the latter who are *equally* responsible for the collateral damage that is visited upon their communities due to the retaliation carried out by the other side. Some would go so far as to say that they bear prime responsibility to the extent that it could constitute deliberate provocation for inducing massive retaliation of a type that would further alienate the population against a strong foe.

There are as many dimensions to terrorism as there are for the causes of terrorism. Like in the case of national security where dimensions other than the military - like economic strength, internal cohesion, governance modes, regional and international environment and so on - have to be taken into account, similarly the term terrorism has loosely come to embrace in people's minds other forms like state terrorism and economic terrorism. The latter, it is said, is being perpetrated by the haves on the have-nots and, more importantly, by the Western nations on the developing nations. There is merit in these arguments. However, in accepting the merit of the argument care has to be taken that it does not obfuscate the issue to the extent that the fight against global terrorism, as manifested in the September 11 attacks or the attack on the Indian Parliament in New Delhi December 13, 2001 and Mumbai in November 2008 (26/11) is compromised thereby.

There is no doubt that millions around the world have died of starvation and hunger due to natural calamities as also manmade economic policies – at the national as well as global levels; resulting in many more deaths and retarded growth than all the acts of terrorism put together. It is, however, not the same thing as wanton violence against innocent civilians for pursuing political ends. Direct, palpable violence leading to death and destruction due to the wantonness and callousness of the act attributable to a set of individuals cannot be bracketed with the suffering endured by the deprived sections of society due to policy decisions taken by governments over a period of time, especially if the governments happen to be elected governments functioning under democratic dispensations. Such policies may become the cause of social unrest, which in turn could lead to terrorism as the means to effecting changes in these policies. Nevertheless, they do not justify terror induced through acts of violence on civilians and innocent bystanders.

While enacting legislation to deal with acts of terrorism an insuperable problem to date has been the lack of acceptability of common definition of terrorism, at the national and the global levels. This writer had attempted to overcome this lacuna by constructing a shunt around the definitional impasse because it would be virtually impossible to get unanimity on this count, not only at the international level but within the country as well. How does one explain that while a certain type of legislation to deal with security threats has been enacted in one state and sanctioned by the government and signed into law by the President, it continues to be rejected when sent to the Centre for ratification by another state (Gujarat). How can the Supreme Court remain a silent bystander to such obvious political discord between parties, as they lose sight of the overriding concern for national security. The book *Dealing with Global Terrorism: The Way Forward* has a chapter *'Finding a Way Through the Definitional Labyrinth'*. It could be examined by the legislative bodies in the country in order to give greater teeth to the law enforcement agencies for dealing with a menace that seems to grow worse with each passing year.

The Judicial Perspective

One can begin by posing a simple question to the eminent justices of the Supreme Court and the High Courts. The Maoists in the red belt have been using IED and planting land mines to blow up vehicles. They have been indulging in other acts of terror. Similarly, the jihadis from across the border and their affiliates within the country have indulged in equally gruesome acts. While the laws of the land do not differentiate between the first category and the second should the yardstick for dealing with them be the same. This is a question that merits consideration. When the laws are applied to the perpetrators of these crimes there may not be any great differentiation on the face of it. However, there is a fundamental difference. The Maoists in the red belt are home grown opponents who have an alternative vision for the development of the adivasis and backward classes on whose behalf they have taken up an armed struggle against the state, essentially the government of the day. They would like to bring about a change in government through the bullet, if necessary. They are not anti-India per se. They do not have any desire to see India destroyed. In the case of the jihadis their motto has been death to the Hindus and non-believers, i.e., Jews and Christians. They seek the destruction or diminishment of India. Therefore, when dealing with these two categories of violators the difference in their motivation should not be lost sight of. There can be grounds for leniency in the category falling under the Maoist umbrella. The aspect of human rights might find some favour in this category. On the other hand human rights cannot be a major consideration for elements whose *raison d'etre* is the killing of kafirs and the destruction of the Indian state.

Inaction, passive resistance, or waiting for something to happen before retaliating, even when sufficient instances of the deadly nature of the peril have already come to light allows the enemies of society to choose their moment, i.e.

time, place and the target. It is tantamount to perpetually ceding the initiative. When the former have all the time in the world to choose the target and the time and place for striking, the chances are that they would be able to succeed, irrespective of the security measures adopted.

Therefore, the call for preventive action will become more persistent in one state after another that is being subjected to terrorist attacks, especially when these attacks are motivated by religious differences on a global scale, as opposed to limited actions confined to a particular region or between one state and its neighbouring state.

6

FOUNTAINHEAD OF CORRUPTION

RECONCILING COALITION DHARMA, GOOD GOVERNANCE AND NATIONAL SECURITY

The 2009 elections were considered a landmark in several ways. Once the results came in the collective sigh of relief from a large majority of the Indian population was audible across the length and breadth of the country.

The prospect of a stable government at the Centre after the months-long prognostication of fractured coalitions based on Third and Fourth Fronts with any number of other strange combinations thrown in for good measure was indeed a welcome relief. Quite possibly the dread of unholy alliances without any pretense to good government had conveyed itself to the electorate. While welcoming the results there is a need to examine as to how this landmark election that paved the way for governance stability came about. To recapitulate a few aspects:

- The conduct of elections for an electorate of 700 million voters, 400 million of which were exercising their franchise can be deemed to be remarkable by any reckoning.
- In many respects the exercise can be said to have been unique, practically almost impossible to replicate on this scale elsewhere.
- Since T.N. Seshan became the Chief Election Commissioner about 15 years ago and showed the power that inhered in the Election Commission (EC) under the Constitution the EC has grown from strength to strength. Of course, such was the

unfettered authority that Mr. Seshan vested in himself that an alarmed government had to appeal to the Supreme Court, which decided to make the Commission a 3-member body. Nevertheless the EC since the Seshan days has developed institutional vigour. It has won the respect of the electorate for holding 'freer and fairer' elections, even the grudging respect of the political parties.

- By now such is the stature of the Election Commission that political parties that were ruling the roost as part of UPA-I government (i.e., the first UPA government from 2004 to 2009) and have got decimated this time around have meekly accepted the people's verdict. Nobody has seriously made the charge of 'rigging'. This has to be compared with the turmoil in Iran after the latest presidential election and the unrest that follows election results in many other countries, not excluding the USA and the controversy in Florida that brought Mr. George W. Bush to the White House in January 2001.
- It is thus a fitting tribute to the maturing of Indian democracy and the respect that the Election Commission has earned for itself within the country and around the world.
- Since it has become one of the strongest pillars of Indian democracy it has to be seen to that the government ensures that Election Commissioners are persons of exceptional merit and intellectual honesty.
- Therefore, the new government should follow the time-hallowed practice of selecting the best persons of irreproachable character and probity in consultation with the leader of the opposition.
- Similarly, retired Election Commissioners must not be given plum government positions for at least 10 years after retiring. In fact, such should be the

strength of character of the Election Commissioners that even if offered tempting post-retirement sinecures, they should refuse. Unfortunately, this has not happened.

- In the 2009 elections – both at the centre and for the state assemblies that went to vote – the results have been termed as a 'watershed' by most political analysts and commentators.

Wisdom of Rural India

But how did this result that brought a 'collective sigh of relief' across the length and breadth of the country come about. If one were to examine the composition of the 400 million or so voters who cast their votes it would be seen that the large majority of them, possibly over 80 percent, were from among the weaker segments of society, the lower middle class, the semi-destitute and most of them below the poverty line (BPL voters). As a guess based on inputs gleaned from the media it can be assumed that the depressed classes – the have-nots of society – generally turned out in full strength or very large numbers to cast their vote. The same unfortunately cannot be said about the middle class – the more affluent sections, the haves. Their voting percentage seldom exceeds 25 percent on an average; actually it may be lower. From the foregoing analysis one comes to the ineluctable conclusion that the so-called unlettered backwards constitute the backbone of Indian democracy, physically by their sheer mass as well as for their commitment to democracy. They are rooted in India's soil. Their better-off upper crust brethren are more part of the new market-capitalised global fraternity that leaves much the heaviest footprint on the fast depleting resources of the planet. It is the former who, yet again, displayed the rare wisdom to give India governance stability not only at the Centre, but practically in all the states where assembly elections were simultaneously held. Is there a lesson in this, which both the government and India's wealth producers should take note of.

Now after the self-congratulatory bouquets it behooves us to discern the dark clouds on the horizon. The elections were staggered over a period of several weeks. Why was that necessary? Of late it has become almost mandatory to deploy central paramilitary forces in fairly large numbers to ensure that there is no booth capturing or voter intimidation. The geographical spread of the country and the remoteness of some of the areas make it very difficult, if not impossible, to deploy paramilitary forces and independent election observers in requisite numbers simultaneously all over the country. This mode of conduct of elections at the national level has come to stay, at least for the foreseeable future. Why should that be the case? In a manner of speaking isn't it only a step away from conducting national elections under the aegis of the Army?

The reason is that throughout the country, almost without exception, there is misgiving about the competence, impartiality or neutrality of the state law and order and governance machineries. It is a severe indictment of local police and bureaucracy. Many chief ministers go out of the way to appoint partisan police officers and civil servants in certain constituencies prior to the elections. In fact, such was the ire of one of the chief ministers in the recent elections that several police officers and district magistrates were summarily transferred, as a punishment, where the chief minister's party lost. In other words they were made to pay for not having sufficiently interfered with the conduct of free and fair elections. Even after this outrageous action, completely lacking in even elementary governance finesse, the CM got away with it without the Governor, the High Court or the Centre asking for an explanation. Ultimately the Supreme Court appears to have asked for an explanation based on a Public Interest Litigation (PIL). In sum, the constitutional authorities that justifiably could have intervened chose to look the other way. Why, because the conduct of practically every political party leaves much to be desired.

Criminalisation of the Polity

Inevitably one is faced with the grim reality that the political parties – practically one and all – have contributed solidly to the criminalization of the polity. They have started giving tickets – approved at the highest levels of the concerned parties – to known criminals, notorious for their gangsterism, voter intimidation and even elimination of troublesome opponents. Their cases continue to languish in the courts for years, even decades. It would not be wrong to say that the political parties have joined hands to usher in 'robust gangsterism' into the political process - pre-election, during elections and post-election. The Election Commission as well as the Judiciary appear to have become listless bystanders of this mass rape of democracy. What are the consequences of this seeming indifference on the part of those who have the power under the Constitution to set matters right. According to some studies, as compared to the year 2004, the number of MPs with criminal records has gone up. In the 2004 Lok Sabha, there were 128 MPs out of which 55 had serious criminal records and now there are 153 MPs with 74 having serious criminal charges against them. Thus, there is an increase of about 17.2 per cent in MPs with criminal records and 30.9 per cent increase in the numbers of MPs with serious criminal records. Both the Congress and the BJP are studded with 43 and 41 such MPs respectively. Out of these, Uttar Pradesh has maximum MPs with criminal cases (total of 31 out of which 22 have serious charges against them). Maharashtra is second with 23 MPs having criminal cases out of which 9 have serious cases against them. It is followed by Bihar, Andhra Pradesh and Gujarat. The criminalization of politics has become an extremely big concern. Even the numbers of MPs with serious criminal cases has gone up. The biggest reason for this seems to be the undemocratic and autocratic selection and nomination of candidates by political parties. Money and muscle power has become the electoral *dharma* of the political parties, the two largest among them, so-called main national parties, turning out to be the biggest agents for the criminalisation of the polity and, by extension the entire process of governance. To put it another way, they are steeped in *adharma*.

In India most people understand the meaning of the word *dharma*. Very simply it can be explained as: "*Dharma* means every ideal which we can propose to ourselves and the law of its working out". Of course, in this country the Karmic consequences of *adharma* are fairly well understood by most people, although the lust for power and short-term gains makes them lose sight of where their true interests should lie. Democracies work on traditions and conventions; however, a parliament with as many as 25 percent MPs with criminal backgrounds will certainly not be one that respects ethics, morality and democratic norms. It then becomes self-evident that '*adharma*' has crept into the DNA of the new parliament, as was the case in the earlier parliament. As to how much of the '*adharma*' creeps into government functioning will depend almost solely on the authority of the Prime Minister and his 'desire' or ability to express that authority seeing that many of his ministers have a background that puts them in the 'unsavoury'category.

Manmohan's Day

To amplify, in the previous government, in coalition UPA-I, the Prime Minister's office, whatever anyone may say, lacked true authority. He was 'appointed' by the party leader as were several of his cabinet colleagues who did not show sufficient deference to him as should be the case in any cabinet system. This time around victory of the Congress Party is attributable to a considerable degree to Dr. Manmohan Singh himself. The nation has vested Dr. Manmohan Singh with a stature and authority that would be the envy of many leaders. The mandate is his, in the first instance, to restore "dharma". The rest will automatically follow. It needs to be reiterated that in 2009 the Prime Ministership was not bequeathed to Dr. Manmohan Singh as it was in 2004. He is now the Prime Minister of India due to the assertion of the national will. The mandate is his as much as that of his party. From here on, the failure to raise the moral and ethical standard of the government will be directly at his doorstep. In the light of the foregoing the first 'order of the day' for the PM should be to work towards the amendment of the Representation of People Act to exclude criminals from becoming legislators. A simple amendment to the affect that 'any one against whom a court of law - not the prosecution or the executive - has framed criminal charges would be ineligible'. For no matter how improved the government functioning, the stench of criminality and, by extension, corruption from the legislative bodies pervades the land.

Their numbers - of legislators with criminal backgrounds-has become so large that taking into account the state assemblies their combined strength exceeds the strength of any single political party. Taking the argument a step further, should a rallying cry go out for all legislators with criminal backgrounds to unite in casting their vote in the electoral college for the election of the next President or Vice President, they could materially affect the outcome. So pervasive is the corrupting influence of legislators with criminal backgrounds, more so in the state assemblies where collectively their numbers might at some stage give them a simple majority in the legislature, that it is one of the biggest threats to national security. This threat being from "within" the system becomes even more insidious. If not 'yet' at the centre to the same extent, in the states the criminal-politician-bureaucrat nexus has become so entrenched that even when elements from the underworld, suspected as being amenable to infiltration from outsiders with anti-national motivation, are identified, the state police either feels helpless to act against them or puts their cases on the back burner because they have become too powerful to be proceeded against. Many such examples have surfaced from time to time in the national media. In the regional media journalists are routinely intimidated and even eliminated.

It should be understood that in many of the states the inroads made by anti-social and anti-national elements into the state government organisations are so deep that good governance has become virtually non-existent for large segments of the population. It is perhaps the single most contributory factor to the rise of 'naxalism' and 'maoism' in many districts of India. Who then is responsible for this state of affairs? To a man the blame for it rests almost entirely with the political parties and their fatal embrace with the criminal elements that they have taken to their bosoms. In the case of some regional parties the leaders of the political parties themselves have several cases against them. They have become chief ministers and home ministers, in charge of police and state intelligence forces. The rot is already too deep. There was a case, several years ago where a legislator with several criminal cases, including murder, against him was being strongly recommended for becoming the Home Minister or Minister of State for Home at the centre. By now it should have become clear that in several states of the union a point has been reached that the damage is almost beyond repair. Occasionally judicial intervention keeps the system from completely going under. Remedial action by the Centre to restore good governance and the rule of law is nowhere in sight. Again the reason is that the two major national parties, the Congress and the BJP are themselves hopelessly complicit in the unholy nexus mentioned earlier on. Just make a tally of the number of people with criminal backgrounds to whom these two parties have given tickets for the Lok Sabha election 2009; add to that the tickets given for elections to state legislatures, the figures become much too high. They can no longer shy away from their role in the spread of corruption and decline in governance and law and order across the country.

Amidst this dismal narration the ordinary, largely unlettered Indian voter, thanks to the impartial conduct of elections by the Election Commission has given the country another chance with a decisive mandate for stability and good governance to get rid of the corroding influences that have crept into the political parties and the legislatures. It is to be noted that while the numbers of legislators with criminal backgrounds may have gone up, some of the most notorious and entrenched mafia-like dons in UP and Bihar, after decades of ruling the roost through terror and voter intimidation, have had their comeuppance in the 2009 elections; almost entirely due to the sagacity of the voter and the tough no-nonsense approach of the Election Commission. The voters have not only given a stable governing majority at the Centre, they have repeated the pattern in all the state assemblies where elections were held.

Judicial Reforms

To sum up this part of the presentation it can be said that the 'foremost' duty of the Prime Minister and his government is to enact the necessary legislation to bring in an enabling environment for the expression of good government, restoration of law and order for the common man and the rooting out of corruption. The situation today is that even the most laudable programmes of the government do not reach the beneficiaries because the instrumentalities of the state for delivering the benefits at the end of the chain have been thoroughly corrupted or blunted. No doubt there are plenty of civil servants and police officers who remain uncorrupted. It is they who are carrying on the business of governance and have prevented the system from complete collapse. Their numbers, however, are fast dwindling. In the light of the above the foremost legislative priority before the Manmohan Singh government should be:

- Amendment to the RPA as explained earlier.

- Completing the Police Reforms as ordained by the Supreme Court; and setting up of the National Judicial Council and the Judicial Accountability Council.
- Ensuring that key institutions like the Election Commission, the CBI and the Central Vigilance Commission remain totally insulated from political interference. Only the Prime Minister is in a position to ensure the agenda outlined above. He must act swiftly and decisively to reassure the public that he means business.

All the legislative exercises mentioned above should be followed through on overriding priority. In any case, they should stand implemented, latest by 31 December 2009 – in the year of the mandate that revived the hope of Indians that the country could be well on the way to good governance and inclusive growth for all; the former being a prerequisite for the latter.

National Security

In the last part, the presentation goes into an aspect of National Security that is on occasion subtly, even surreptitiously, undermined without the public at large, or even the coalition members, being aware that decisions being taken on behalf of the government in the field of foreign affairs were being made without reference to the rest of the cabinet or ministers of the coalition partners. In the two cases cited below they were made, more on the spur of the moment, violating the principle of collective responsibility of the party heading the coalition, or the coalition partners. In short, not enough evaluation was carried out as to their long-term ramifications for the country. What is worse they were not even brought before the CCS for clearance. The first item relates to the unilateral abrogation of the 1972 ABM Treaty by George W. Bush not long after coming to the White House. Of course the new president rejected many other protocols leading to consternation around the world. It would be recalled that the ABM Treaty between the USA and Soviet Union (later on Russia as the successor state) was the linchpin of the global security architecture after the fall of the Berlin Wall and the dissolution of the Soviet Union. Besides keeping a check on the billions of dollars being poured into Star Wars technologies, the Treaty essentially prevented open militarization of space.

The whole world – East and West – favoured the Treaty, India more so than others for reasons that would generally be well known. Nevertheless, almost immediately after the announcement being made in Washington, the MEA endorsed it whole-heartedly, taking the US media and the world by surprise at the speed at which India's long-held position was overturned. Similar dismay was expressed in the Indian press. A cartoonist even showed the US flag flying on MEA vehicles. Needless to say, that neither the Cabinet nor the CCS and CCPA were consulted before the declaration from New Delhi. The coalition partners remained totally oblivious till much later. There was a suggestion by one of the commentators that somebody was personally trying to curry favour with the new US administration. Whatever be the case, it lowered India's image in the eyes of the world.

Iran Issue

The second instance is more recent. One fine day in 2007 practically the entire media in India as well as foreign policy veterans were shocked to learn that the previous day India had voted against Iran at the IAEA board meeting in Vienna. The amazement in Iran was palpable at every street corner. The reason being that since the visit of the foreign minister Sardar Swaran Singh to Tehran, followed by the visit of Smt. Indira Gandhi in 1974 relations between Iran and India had improved considerably. After that memorable opening the two countries started moving together in the economic field and India's views carried weight in Tehran, as would be confirmed by diplomats posted to that country from that time onward. Besides the obvious energy security provided by a close neighbour in the region the two countries had been cooperating in Afghanistan along with Russia. India's connectivity to Central Asia through the only country whose assistance was available received a boost. Geopolitically it was crucial for India to remain friendly with Iran. Regardless as to how India felt about Iran's quest for advanced nuclear technologies prior to the Vienna vote or post-facto after the deed was done, India's geo-strategic imperative for a friendly Iran can hardly be denied. India could have abstained, in spite of the US pressure. After the casting of the negative vote relations between the two countries have taken a downturn. The Iranian government, irrespective of the hue, no longer trusts India. The image of the country of India's size has also taken a hard knock. India cannot be trusted to take an independent stand was the feeling that swept the region, the pat on the back from the Western world and USA notwithstanding. However, without going into the long-term consequences of that fateful decision the fact remains that it was again not a collegiate decision. The Cabinet, CCS, CCPA or the coalition partners were not consulted. Had these entities been consulted it can be stated with reasonable certainty that the collective decision would have been to abstain rather than cast a negative vote against Iran in Vienna under pressure from the Americans.

By hindsight the consensus would be that both were hasty and wrong decisions. However, in raising this issue the aim is not merely to discuss the correctness of the decisions or otherwise. The point being highlighted is that due process was not followed and due diligence was not carried out by experts, even in-house experts. The basis of the conduct of government in a coalition or even a single party government is the concept of collective responsibility of the cabinet. Not only in the field of foreign policy, even in the case of decisions that constitute drastic departure from existing policies, the reference to the CCS and the CCPA, where applicable, has to be mandatory. This principle should become sacrosanct.

The principle of collective responsibility where critical issues are at stake must become inviolable hereafter. It should invariably be the collegium that should weigh and collectively decide on such very weighty matters. In both the coalition governments, the NDA government headed by Mr. Vajpayee and UPA I, headed by Dr. Manmohan Singh the collegium was given the go-by, sometimes even the PM was given the go-by. This elementary principle of governance which is the cornerstone of parliamentary democracy must never be allowed to be violated with impunity in UPA II and all governments that follow.

Time for PM to Act

Governments in the past have shown a strong penchant for shying away from reforms that enhance transparency, curb corruption at the higher levels of government or other legislative measures that would improve accountability. Some of the most urgent measures like amendment to the RPA, Police reforms and strengthening of the independence of the CBI, CVC and allied investigative agencies have been spelt out. The personnel deficiencies of many of these agencies have also to be made up on top priority. The other burning issues before the government, again in order of priority, relate to the setting up of the National Judicial Commission and the administrative reforms recommended by the Moily Committee.

The government of Dr. Manmohan Singh should not hesitate to bring in the above-mentioned reforms at the earliest. The combined strength of the Congress and BJP comes up to 322; with just one or two of the major allies they are in a position to drum up a two-third majority for enacting the type of legislation that could take the country to the front ranks of well governed nations. The voters have spoken. The ball is squarely in the court of Dr. Manmohan Singh.

[Based on talk delivered at the India International Centre in 2009]

COURT ON PIL

[MRGG petition to the Chief Justice of the Supreme Court]

In the PIL on the subject the petitioner has prayed that the statutory provision mandating sanction for prosecuting politicians and public servants be dispensed with. In this regard several documents having a direct bearing on the subject are attached herewith. Some of these are copies of letters already placed before the Hon'ble Justices dealing with similar cases in the past. If considered pertinent, the MRGG correspondence can be impleaded, being material to the case under consideration. In addition to the self-evident aspect of the 'single directive' dealing a body blow to equality before the law for citizens of the country, the issue of national security, which is linked to it, assumes overriding importance. Seeing the percentage of criminals that have entered the legislative process at the Centre and in the States and the fact that their strength keeps increasing with each passing year there is an ineluctable need for the Courts to now give a ruling, the spirit of which can *never* be tampered with by vested interests bent upon subverting the letter as well as the spirit of such rulings.

In spite of having admitted in the Supreme Court that the nexus among criminals, politicians and bureaucrats has increased, leading to a 'disturbingly' high level of corruption, the UPA Government has opposed any move to strike down the "Single Directive" in the Central Vigilance Commission (CVC), that protected top officials from direct investigation by the CBI. Many arguments have already been put forward in articles appearing in leading dailies opposing the single directive. In referring the issue of the single directive to a Constitution Bench to decide whether the "arbitrariness" of the law could be a ground to strike it down, the Court appears to have been concentrating mainly on the aspect of arbitrariness *per se*. It is the opinion of this writer that several other equally weighty issues merit consideration. These are spelled out in the ensuing paragraphs.

The most important of these relates to the aspect of national security. Instances can be cited where the national interest has been subverted for extraneous considerations. In the majority of cases of this kind, had the officials been properly investigated, *in time,* it would have revealed that the decision-making had been influenced wholly, or to a significant degree, by interests working at the behest of elements inimical to India. That being the case, it is very much on the cards that the single directive is being used or could be used by these very interests to blackmail officials for ensuring that the bureaucrat covered by the single directive and the political figure heading the ministry continue to toe the line. Over a period of time the practice could undermine the country's security without the nation being any the wiser. The continuance of the coverage of rogue elements under the single directive could end up by weakening the nation's stability, defensibility or viability. Only recently, it was averred by a former Governor, Reserve Bank of India, that many of the decisions taken by the top echelons of government were not in the national interest. If such a distinguished, high-ranking person is impelled to come out with a statement of this nature it would imperil the safety of the nation, if note were not to be taken by the highest judicial body in the land.

The next aspect to be taken into account is that of *reductio ad absurdum.* Once arbitrariness of this nature at the highest level of governance is allowed to go unchallenged there would be nothing to prevent the State Governments to follow suit. Thereafter, the armed forces could start clamouring for similar exemptions for brigadiers and above. They would, in turn, be followed by the paramilitary forces, by which time the Constitution itself would be ready for a decent burial.

Adding to the strangeness of the government's stand is the bizarre contention that fear of CBI investigation would prevent senior officials from taking decisions. This is as specious a plea as any. Why did this fear not obtain before the Narasimha Rao era, which had become synonymous with political skullduggery?

It is possible to go on in this vein. A very serious matter has languished for much too long without being set right.

There is a marked trend among political circles to erode the authority of the Supremg Court of India, the highest judicial body under the Constitution. It is a trend, which if not checked, could lead to the end of governance, that is already faltering, and, in fact, much of the civilised existence that the country has generally enjoyed in the last sixty years, even if the benefits have not yet trickled down to those below the poverty line. The lack of 'trickle down' is also directly attributable to the politicians and the ruling class. The amounts that have been sanctioned under various central schemes add up to astronomical sums. As is well known, since Rajiv Gandhi first articulated it, the monies are siphoned off by the political class (fodder, Taj and other scams of a similar nature are just a few in the public eye). The aggrandisement of the political class – and some bureaucrats as well - has to be seen to be believed. It is mind boggling. And now they are benefiting their henchmen through MPLADS. On top of that they have the temerity to tell non-governmental entities that the latter are not making sufficient effort toward affirmative action.

In sum, the polity has brought the country to its knees through misgovernance, self-aggrandisement, hypocrisy, vote bank politics, casteism, right wing excesses, tampering with and undermining national security, malfeasance, misfeasance, defalcation, criminalising of the polity, undermining of the judiciary and ......and.............The list is endless.

If the bulk of the political class is not strung up from the lamp posts on Raisina Hill or lynched by the public it is not because of the gun-toting security that they have surrounded themselves with from the national exchequer at the cost of national security. They are shielded from public wrath by the very Courts that they are trying to now undermine. It is high time that the NGOs and the non-agitating, law-abiding, tax paying citizens came out to make it clear to the political elements that they would not stand for undermining the majesty of the highest courts. With great difficulty, after a nearly irredeemable national decline, Pakistan has finally been able to restore the primacy of the highest judicial body, albeit only tentatively so far. Here in India, the rogue elements, mainly the political class (with many honourable exceptions), are the ones who are attempting to create chaos.

All concerned citizens must immediately make their views known through the print and electronic media as well as writing to the Honourable Justices for letting them know that the law-abiding public, the overwhelming majority of Indians, fully support their attempts to restore public morality, good governance and an element of sanity in the conduct of national affairs. The Courts would be well within their rights to order stiff prison sentences for those who openly defy them for the sake of vote bank politics. Even a body like the MCD can be put under temporary receivership should it continue to defy court directives.

SKEWED DEBATE

The manner in which parliament is debating, examining and passing legislation, often in indecent haste, and often to benefit serving members, could erode the very future of Indian democracy if corrective action is not taken at the earliest.

Nor should the government be allowed to get away with pronouncements or follow up action that smacks of opportunism and which can be shown to be against the interest of the country, i.e., action which only interests inimical to the country could wish upon the country. An example is the announcement by the government to immediately double or considerably enhance the capacity of elite institutions and other educational institutions.

The infeasibility of the proposition has already been commented upon by various educators and eminent persons. What has not been adequately commented upon is the effect that hasty increases or capacity doubling can have on the institutional vigour or the character and global reputations of temples of educational excellence established over a lifetime or lifetimes by devoted administrators and teachers of yesteryear. No institution of repute imparting high quality education in any field can withstand a sudden, unplanned influx based on a government fiat of the nature being planned by the present government. It could end up by destroying the competence and character of the institution.

The question then arises: "Are the hundreds of legislators backing the government's nationally injurious actions not aware of the implications of these actions"? If they are unaware are they competent to legislate, and that to in a tearing hurry, without listening to expert bodies and examining the proposals with reasonable diligence, if not due diligence? On the other hand if they are aware and have fallen silent, the only conclusion that can be drawn is that the country has already fallen into the hands of interests inimical to India.

These inimical interests have mastered the art of vote bank politics with pocket or 'wrotten burroughs' based on slumlords and mafias in slums which they will not allow the courts to displace by enacting ordinances and legislations to set aside court judgments. A large number of them have criminal backgrounds with files on them held by intelligence agencies that more than hint at hostile foreign backing. Most other legislators do "not" represent their constituencies in the true sense of the word having come into parliament with as little as 20 or 25 percent votes, sometimes even less.

Civil society, concerned citizens and the courts have to take a fresh look at the erosion of democracy and the threat to the constitution by the activities of people currently occupying the highest legislative and executive positions in the land.

The right to equality already stands eroded. None or very few of the criminal cases against legislators have been completed in time or the guilty party brought to book. As a first step, the highest Court should suo motu direct that an independent prosecuting authority, answerable directly to the Court, take over all pending prosecutions and complete them in given time frames, if not before the next parliamentary elections. Meanwhile, all such legislators, under a cloud, must not get a free hand to further degrade democratic norms. It is for the public to mount a counter offensive, here and now.

7

BLACK MONEY

"Idhar Udhar Ki Baat Mat Kar,
Yeh batla Kafila Kisne loota"

THE NEW MONSTER

"Government accountability has to be highlighted on the way they have gone about retrieving black money information in the past. A scrutiny of their letters, that the SC can demand to see, would perhaps undoubtedly show that letters from Swiss authorities seeking clarifications have remained unanswered for inordinately long periods, thereby tacitly indicating to the other side the disinclination of the GoI to proceed further. Additionally, letters seeking information have been said to have contained deliberate errors, omissions and the like knowing that the Swiss authorities would reject them, thus deliberately further delaying the process. In all such cases the incumbents authorising the drafts have to be made known to the Court and the public and brought to book. These areas are ones where the government ineptitude and subversion of the process will get clearly highlighted. The SC must be told that there is danger to national security as forces inimical to the country may have entered the innards of the government to wreck it from within. The cumulative evidence simply cannot be ignored".

"The powers that be, are saying that while taking the decision on the CVC, the case against him was not made known to them. Firstly, nobody believes this statement. However, the more deadly aspect relates to national security.

In case they are not dissembling, is the government fit to run the country. Are important decisions at the highest levels concerning India's critical interests also being taken in this cavalier fashion. Another aspect to be considered is, 'when they say the government cannot divulge the lists of the black money holders who exactly are the government'. In this UPA II coalition it can be wagered that the information is only with the Congress Party; and the apex, the Maximum Leader, not part of the government would also have the list without doubt, including closest advisers and the coterie. Is the list then being used to blackmail, make people conform and the like. Have elements inimical to the country also become privy to state secrets. The danger to national security is immediate. Stop pussyfooting. Tell it like it is. Are the lists being used to make those on the list cough up or support the party? Are the lists being tampered with? Who are the custodians? Do the Reserve Bank and Enforcement Directorate, CVC, CBI have the lists? Who else is privy to them? The implications are grave. Do the needful, here and now".

The next extract has been taken from the Pakistani paper *"The News"* dated January 26, 2011, reproduced in *The Indian Express*, New Delhi, dated January 29, 2011, Page #15:

Taking suo motu notice of corruption in a government insurance company, a bench headed by the chief justice of Pakistan, Iftikhar Muhammad Chaudhry was quoted as saying "The culture of not arresting big fish should end, adding that plundering the national wealth has become routine practice, which needed to be stopped forthwith. 'Thieves have gathered to save thieves'". (Unquote)

As distinct from the neighboring country that is increasingly being referred to as a 'failed state' India is, or should be, a functioning democracy. However, the remarks attributed to the Chief Justice of Pakistan could very well be applied to the conditions obtaining at the highest levels of government in New Delhi. Concerned citizens and informed opinion throughout the country is increasingly apprehensive that the extra-constitutional authority vesting in the Chairperson of the UPA could perhaps be exercising a mafia-like stranglehold on the functioning of the government, as becomes apparent from the emails reproduced above. In the process, practically every investigative agency and allied institution, whose independent and competent functioning become the cornerstone of national security and good governance have been subverted and rendered ineffective. Numerous upright functionaries have been sidelined and those willing to act on the signals emanating from the extra-constitutional authority have been promoted to the highest posts. It has affected the morale and eroded the credibility of the said agencies. Should the stranglehold being exercised from without, possibly by elements inimical to the country that might have infiltrated the system, be allowed to continue for even a little while longer the damage to democracy in India and the country's security might become much too great for comfort.

Since the danger is real and immediate, and the public clamour against corruption and lack of accountability at the highest levels of government continues to grow, it would be in the fitness of things for the Honorable Supreme Court, instead of 'agonizing' over the deteriorating situation, to come down very hard on the wrongdoers, with clear directives that would leave no scope for deviation or misinterpretation as has often been the case in the past. The result has been that the situation has actually deteriorated over the years since the earlier judgments that were designed specifically to set things right.

While dealing with contentious matters resting before the Honorable Court, relating to the 2G Scam, appointment of tainted CVC, retrieval of black money and other corruption cases, an ideal opportunity becomes available for issuing the following *supplementary* directives for immediate implementation by the government. These can be summarised as:

(a) In the selection of all constitutional authorities like the CAG, CVC, Chief Election Commissioner and the other Election Commissioners the selecting panel should be expanded by two additional members. One of them could be a sitting judge of the Supreme Court to be nominated each year by the Chief Justice and the other could be the Governor of the Reserve Bank.

(b) Foolproof procedures for ensuring the independent functioning of the CBI and allied agencies of the government, evidently with due regard to the need for overall political supervision in the rarest of rare cases.

(c) The Centre and State governments should be given a fresh date, not later than 31 December 2013, for full implementation of the Supreme Court directives issued earlier on Police reforms, in letter and spirit. In order to ensure compliance this time around an Implementation Commission to be formed under the aegis of the Supreme Court to oversee implementation and monitor functioning for a period of five years. It should be made known to the concerned authorities that infringements or tardiness would be dealt with in exemplary fashion.

(d) Very strict monitoring by an Independent Oversight Panel appointed by the Supreme Court to monitor government action for retrieval of illegal money stashed abroad.

Before a Tunisia or Egypt type situation develops in this country as well, owing to the enormity of corruption and levels at which it is taking place in the government, the public pins its hopes on the Supreme Court to set matters right before democracy is delivered a body blow by the present dispensation and others of like tendencies that might follow should correctives not be applied. The government in its arrogance (bravado based on fear of exposure) has tied itself in knots due to its indefensible actions as well as the equally indefensible arguments being put forward by its representatives. Another historic opportunity of this nature for in-depth reform may not be available to the country in the foreseeable future. The People of India would welcome with joy and hope should the Honorable Supreme Court step in decisively to stem the rot.

Outpourings of Civic Frustration

Leaving aside frivolous cases, many of the PILs before the highest courts are the result of decades of frustration; every channel available to the public to seek redress has been blocked by officials who have become terminally corrupted, secure in the knowledge that the rot having been sanctified at the very top they would automatically enjoy immunity from prosecution; i.e., sanction for prosecution would either not be forthcoming or would be granted so belatedly that enough time would be available for destruction of evidence or even the doing away of witnesses.

In the light of what has been stated above should the judiciary in the highest courts in the country be side-tracked, from what its sees as the greatest challenge to India's democracy, by orchestrated charges of judicial over-activism, Indian democracy may itself become terminally ill. In its fight against the evil that has befallen the land due to the failure of legislatures and the executive, important democracy-strengthening judgments of the highest court have to be seen as attempts to right the ship of state, which is listing dangerously to prevent it from going under. Therefore, at this critical juncture it is of the utmost importance for Their Lordships of the Supreme Court to ensure that investigative and enforcement agencies as well as constitutional authorities are freed from the evil designs of the corruptors once and for all. The wreckers of democracy should no longer be able subvert, undermine or misdirect investigations against the highest level defaulters in the land, who enjoy immunity not even available to sovereigns in many countries.

SHOCKING APATHY OF GOVERNMENT

Enclosed please find MRGG letter dated March 29, 2011 addressed to Honorable Justice S.H. Kapadia, Chief Justice of India. It is a follow up to the letters sent earlier on black money and blackmail (copies also enclosed). It is becoming increasingly apparent to MRGG, NNFI (National Network for India), Common Cause, ADR and many like-minded civil society organisations fighting for good governance that the government is not really interested in getting to the bottom of the black money trail or the plethora of scams that have surfaced in the last few months. There are bound to be many more that have yet to see the light of day. In spite of strictures by the highest courts the government and its representatives appearing before the Court continue to obfuscate, dissimulate and prevaricate. As if the dismay expressed by the honorable justices from time to time were not enough there could not be a more severe indictment of the government than the interview given by the Ambassador of Switzerland (published in *Mint,* March 29, 2011 on page #4). Relevant excerpts are reproduced below: **"Switzerland's ambassador to India, Philippe Welti, said India has not done enough to obtain information from his country's banks on money laundering despite the public outrage over it. It was not "fair" to see Swiss lenders as protecting criminals by not co-operating with Indian law enforcement agencies, Welti said on Monday. India must file "legitimate requests" with Swiss authorities for banks to release data on illegitimate money allegedly stashed away in numbered accounts, he said. "Check with your government how many requests have been filed," Welti said. "I don't want to say more."** Unquote

The public at large is at its wits end as to how to force the government to ward off the threat to national security by its acts of omission and commission. On the face of it, it appears that interests inimical to the country have taken a stranglehold of the government at the very apex. This mafia-like grip is destroying to the very core large numbers of the top hierarchies of the investigative and enforcement agencies that should be the natural protectors of national security and efficient functioning of democracy. Unless the courts intervene decisively, the emerging threats referred to above could undermine the sanctity of the country and its institutions.

8

BURNING ISSUES

REGIONAL DISPARITY IN THE NORTH-EAST

Very early on it became evident that under-development and unrest in the North-East is to a large extent the result of the Central Government having abdicated its basic sovereign duty for the last fifty years. What is being referred to is the Central Government's inability to keep the Lines of Communication open for all the states of the North-East. In its absence the common man in the States at the periphery is harassed no end and the States suffer heavy losses due to lengthy disruptions to the road and rail networks. They cannot preserve perishable goods when the communications are cut without notice; nor are they in a position to plan as to when these would be restored. It is for this very reason that industrialists are hesitant to invest in the North-East because uncertainty in the flow of materials can *cripple* any enterprise. Most recently, the Chief Minister of Sikkim threw up his hands in despair, when the National Highway to Sikkim was blocked due to the Gorkha agitation. Earlier, over the years it had been blocked for various periods due to frequent Assam bandhs.

In the light of the foregoing, it is recommended that this matter be *urgently* addressed directly. Concerned Ministries and State Governments should be put on notice that the Centre will no longer tolerate disruption to the national (interstate) lines of communication that result in extreme suffering for states at the periphery; who then remain at the mercy of agitationists and anti-social elements. In fact clear directions should be given by the Ministry of Road Transport and Highways, Home Ministry, DONER and all concerned to the effect that Central forces should invariably – and automatically – step in to restore lines of communications every time these are cut for the reasons outlined above. Irrespective of whether the disruptions result from natural calamities or due to blockage of road and rail transport by anti-social elements or on account of political agitations, they cause untold hardship to people in other states well beyond the remit of the elements causing the disruption.

It is felt that once the Government of India *resumes* its sovereign function to *guarantee* free flow of people, services and goods through surface lines of communication to states at the periphery that have suffered extreme hardship and lack of investment on this very count for over 50 years the situation will improve dramatically, almost overnight, so to say. Peace and prosperity will follow sooner than expected.

DEVELOPING TALIBAN-LIKE TENDENCIES

Because of the coverage given to the British delegation visiting the sites related to the 1857 uprising (Indian War of Independence) you could not have failed to notice the shabby treatment meted out to them in various towns of UP. While the administration had politely, but firmly, declined some of their requests, it was the BJP led ruffians - other entities reportedly joined in as well - who turned what the visitors hoped would be a memorable visit into a very unwelcome one. Conceivably, the delegation could have shown greater sensitivity. However, a lack of appreciation on the part of the visitors as to how the events of 1857 might be viewed by the people of India cannot be a justification for the boorish behaviour of the mobs, including the attempted desecration of graves in a British cemetery in Lucknow.

Most visitors coming to India generally carry enormous goodwill for the country – as did this British delegation - out of deep respect for its-civilisational heritage. They hoped to draw deeply from India's spiritual well-springs. The outrageous behavior of the wild-eyed hooligans that political parties nurture in their bosoms is a negation of everything that India stands for. Over the years more and more of them have started displaying shockingly similar symptoms. That should be small comfort to you. For the world, the BJP should have represented the finest traditions of Hinduism. Today, some adherents of the party - call them fringe elements if you like – are taking on a Taliban-like veneer. It demonstrates an ugly strain of intolerance that is far-removed from the tenets of Hinduism that have preserved the sanctity of Hindustan through the ages. I seriously recommend that some of the top leaders betake themselves to the Himalayas, to silently introspect on the true meaning of compassion, tolerance and spirituality. India requires strong central parties. Both the BJP and Congress should pause to reflect as to where they are taking the country.

To come back to the British delegation which comprised some former officers of their Rifle Regiment, there were many among them who would be considered distinguished members of any society. Their average age would have been above 60 years. They included historians, bankers, intellectuals and even a curator of a museum. Surely they deserved better treatment; more so, when the Mayor of London is personally leading the celebrations for India's 60th year of Independence to highlight the country's achievements. Something similar is taking place in New York, Berlin and many other cities of the world. The political class must decide soon enough whether they wish to build upon the tremendous achievements that have finally brought recognition to India or negate the efforts of the entrepreneurial class that has given such a boost to the Indian economy. It is to be hoped that the ancient Indian wisdom that is extolled at every national and international forum trickles down to the political hierarchy that leads the country.

There are other examples of growing intolerance. MF H who is over 90 years old is one of India's best known artists. Whatever the insensitivity in painting Indian goddesses he is more patriotic than many of the people who denounce him. The initial protests made the point; they have to stop pillorying him from day to day. The Shiv Sena appears to have taken leave of its senses, as have many like-minded parties with similar inspiration. Why are they hounding Aamir Khan again and again, this time for supposedly showing disrespect to the Indian flag, as supposedly did Narayan Murthy of Infosys. For the average Hindustani both these individuals have brought far more credit to India than the people who denounce them. Please do not attempt to put any Indian citizen beyond the pale. If the party and its more charged up supporters do not mend their ways the chances of the BJP coming back to power at the Centre will recede with each passing year.

9

JAN LOK PAL DEBATE

BEYOND THE 'JAN LOK PAL BILL'

The ferment in India is unmistakable. The upsurge across the length and breadth of the country in response to the call given by Anna Hazare has caught the imagination of the whole world. There have been parallel upsurges in other countries, most notably the Arab Spring or the Jasmine Revolution in the Middle East. However, the spontaneous uprising in India, encompassing people from all walks of life and of all ages, especially the youth, is unique. Everyone in the world is amazed at the peaceful nature of the large gatherings in cities all over India. The frail looking Anna Hazare has united the nation as never before, in recent memory. There is hope that the government in New Delhi and the powers that be will realise that the people will no longer accept the way that the country is being run. The demand is unmistakable: corruption at the very *apex* of government must end; the guilty must be brought to book through streamlined procedures that brook no delay; and the restoration of transparency and accountability at all levels.

While Anna Hazare and his team have concentrated on the Jan Lokpal Bill, it is important to look beyond. Even if the Lokpal Bill that is considered satisfactory by the public at large is passed by the parliament and speedily enacted into law, seeing the nature and breadth of the support generated, it is equally important that Shri Hazare and the leaders on whose each word the public hangs, send out a strong message that reinforces the cleansing that the Jan Lokpal Bill envisages.

The desired spring cleaning at the top or systemic change is unlikely to come about unless those who sit in parliament are not history sheeters and people wedded to self-aggrandisement and nepotism. They have to be people for whom the country comes first, always and every time. Hence, seeing the expectant faces of the young of India who have come out in the hundreds of thousands, if not millions, Anna Hazare and other leaders who have the pulpit have an opportunity to give a clarion call to the youth to the effect that: "the youth of India take a solemn pledge that hereafter they will come out to vote in full force in every election in the country and ensure that the tainted and the corrupt as well as those leaders in New Delhi who have brought the country to such a sorry pass are *never* again allowed to enter the hallowed portals of Parliament." The opportunity to send out this appeal may not come their way again. The concerned leaders must seize the moment to ensure that the higher purpose, beyond the Jan Lokpal Bill, is served for the future of the country.

WHO RUNS INDIA?

The amazing performance of the three government ministers at 1.30 PM (16 August 2011) before the national media, explaining the government's arrest of Anna Hazare has demonstrated to the nation as to why the government is totally adrift. It was an exercise in sophistry, obfuscation, downright untruths, fair sprinkling of half-truths and artful dissemblance. What is more amazing is that an extremely sharp and intelligent Home Minister made statements that could embarass the government for a long time to come. Evidently, the ministers felt that the public whom they were addressing were a bunch of idiots. Going beyond the amazing assertion of the Home Minister that he had no knowledge of the whereabouts of Anna Hazare, here are a few of the evident slips, possibly made out of desperation that no clever lawyer, leave alone the Home Minister of India would have made:

Statement: "If the public is not happy with the police arrests and actions they should go to the courts". This was repeated so frequently in his statement and in answer to questions that concerned citizens would naturally start wondering whether the constant hint at the option of going to the courts was not an artful ploy to pull the government out of the enormous mess that it had created for itself due to its flat-footedness.

Statement: "I repeat that the citizens have the right to take their grievances against the actions of the 'police' to the courts". Very careful wording, in this instance. Not, if they have a grievance or grievances against *government* action, but 'police' action.

Statement: Again repeated a number of times that the police acted on their own and all their actions were independent actions and that the government and the Home Ministry had nothing to do with them. This was followed once more with the advice (drummed in ad nauseam) that the public had the right to seek redressal from the courts. Several observations flow from this. Instead of having the courage of its decisions or non-decisions, the government is making the police the scapegoat should things get out of hand. That they used excessive force, or did not exercise mature judgment (arguments that are standard for politicians who incite the public and then step back when the going gets tough and make the police take the rap. The police officer concerned takes the rap quietly, is suspended for a period of time or transferred till the episode is forgotten by the media. Thereafter the concerned officer is rehabilitated and secretly rewarded in other ways for not exposing the cowardly, scheming neta). More importantly, what is the impression that the Home Minister is conveying. That the courts should intervene at the drop of a hat; that the government has abrogated its responsibility. What has happened to the chain of police command, for example in Delhi, Lt. Governor of Delhi who is in charge of the police, what about the Chief Minister? Has the incumbent no role to play. Lastly, what about the Home Minister himself. Is he a mere bystander. If this is the belief in the government of its responsibility, it explains as to why all the actions that were supposed to be in place for buttressing national security after 9/11 have such glaring loopholes. Keep passing the buck to the police and every other agency involved. The government and the Home Ministry have nothing to do with it.

Statement: 'I assure you that the government has not given *any* directions to the police. They are acting on their "own".' God forbid that this statement be true. The situation created by Anna Hazare's proposed fast could in the extreme bring the government down, or at the very minimum damage the Congress Party very badly, besides the loss of credibility. That neither the government or its main functionary for law and order, nor the Lt. Governor, advised the police stretches credulity to the limit. Nobody believes it, really. The recent case of 13/7 in Mumbai and the unseemly wrangle between the CM and the Maharashtra Home Minister, with the former accusing the latter of not discharging his duty properly puts paid to the strenuous assertion made by the Home Minister and his cabinet colleagues who blithely kept on reinforcing each other's statements. For a moment suppose that they were true, and were the people of India to take the statement at face value, the implications are horrendous. Here is a situation with ramifications that could affect the government and the country and the Home Minister washes his hands off all responsibility: "The police will decide, it is for them to make the decisions".

Similar dissimulations from the other ministers can be gone into. However, their gravity pales into insignificance compared to the statements referred to above. For the nation it raises fundamental questions about the government's ability to govern or ensure the security of the country. It is inconceivable that nobody in the cabinet had the experience to handle the situation more elegantly. Even the Home Minister is far more able than what emerged at the press conference. The Prime Minister and the cabinet would have been under the impression that the G-4 nominated by the person who appointed the PM in the first place to run the party and the country in her absence would take the critical decisions as ordained. They were out of their depth and hence the hurried interventions of the cabinet.

The reason for the maladroit handling that stares the nation in the face is the manner in which the country is presently being governed. In reality all power is in the hands of a foreign person with full authority and near zero accountability. The Prime Minster, as most of the country suspects is not an independent decision-maker. *The Economist* in a recent issue scathingly referred to the PM as 'the retainer of the Gandhi family'. There was no protest from him or anyone from within the government. Perhaps some hidden mirth on the part of some of his colleagues waiting in the wings to replace him at the behest of the extra-constitutional authority now reportedly convalescing in foreign climes. The country wishes her speedy recovery at a personal level, but for the interest of the country a Supreme Court mandated inquiry should be instituted as to the enormity of the staggering sums that seem to have moved out of the country under the current dispensation and whether it has any chance of being investigated under the same dispensation. For, in essence, that is what the present country-wide agitation is all about.

10

DELHI CITIZENS COMMISSION

PREAMBLE

1. Seeing that

(a) Governance is rapidly declining and corruption in practically all departments of government is increasing equally rapidly;

(b) Functioning and accountability in government departments leaves much to be desired;

(c) Maintenance, Cleanliness, and Upkeep of Delhi's infrastructure, Public Services, Parks, Toilets, Traffic lights, Roads, Pavements and other assets remains far from satisfactory;

(d) Pleas, Petitions, Complaints, Meetings, Citizens groups gatherings and other forms of protest not having yielded results;

(e) Law and order for the common man continues to deteriorate, while those in the government and the political class appropriate the bulk of security and other services that should be available to the public in much larger proportion;

(f) Grievances of the public are seldom addressed;

(g) Accountability at practically all higher levels of governance remains low and non-existent;

(h) The quality of construction and supervision in the build up to the Common Wealth Games (CWG) having brought national shame and heavy loss in public money and the public remaining unconvinced that the culprits at the highest level will be brought to book in reasonable time frames;

(i) That the malaise in practically all categories noticed in the run up to the CWG obtains in most, if not all, ministries, departments and agencies responsible for infrastructure, upkeep, protection of the assets created and the like has generally been of the same abysmal level as that noticed in the build up to the CWG;

(j) Malfeasance, misfeasance, defalcation and large-scale misappropriations at practically all levels of governance having become the order of the day.

2. Several NGOs, RWAs and concerned citizens of Delhi taking it upon themselves to put a stop to what they perceive to be a total lack of accountability and degeneration of governance at practically all levels have come together for the purpose of restoring democratic norms, good governance, improved law and order for the average citizen, probity and accountability in the process of governance in the Capital City of Delhi, as well as at the Centre, since many areas remain under the direct control of the Central government.

AIMS AND OBJECTS

3. The Delhi Citizens Commission (hereafter referred to as Del CC) is being set up with the following Aims and Objects:

(a) To organise and bond the concerned NGOs and RWAs and citizens of Delhi into a potent force for bringing in better governance and improved Law and Order;

(b) To bring about accountability in all government departments and agencies concerned with the capital city and its administration, infrastructure, development, future planning and delivery of services;

(c) To create a functional model along the lines mentioned above for concerned NGOs and Citizens in other states and cities to follow.

COMPOSITION, FUNCTIONING AND CHARTER OF DELHI CITIZENS COMMISSION

Composition

4. The Del CC at its apex will comprise three eminent citizens, whose names in the first instance will be proposed and ratified in a joint conclave comprising Common Cause, NNFI, CHRI, MRGG, FRNV and RWAs and Associates that have combined with the prime movers of the initiative, Common Cause-NNFI-MRGG.

5. In selecting the first set of Del CC commissioners and their subsequent replacement the following aspects will dictate the choice:

(a) The standing, reputation, probity and general competence to discharge their functions should be such that they would be acceptable to the organizations and individuals that have come together for the purpose;

(b) The stature of the Commissioners should be such that they automatically command the respect of the peoples of Delhi and even beyond at the national level;

(c) The Commissioners should be politically neutral in the discharge of their duties;

(d) The Commissioners should have no personal (hidden) agendas nor should they seek or accept awards, positions or high office from the government or any other entity that could tarnish the esteem in which the commissioners would be held;

(e) In principle, the commissioners should generally be free of onerous commitments that could prevent them from devoting adequate time and energies to the task that they would have undertaken.

Charter and Mode of Functioning

6. The commissioners selected by the various NGOs, RWAs and Associates would invariably be persons of great experience, prowess and intellect. They would be the best judges to decide the manner in which they would like to function. The aspects listed below by way of charter and modes of functioning are guidelines that can be improved upon or added to as experience is gained. Briefly, the charter includes, inter alia:

(a) To build up the standing of Del CC so that not only the citizens of Delhi, but the government of Delhi, Central government as well as Parliamentarians, Media and the Judiciary come to recognize and respect the recommendations of the commissioners for all aspects related to promoting good governance, smoother and speedier delivery of services, improvement in law and order, rooting out of corruption and the like;

(b) Based on inputs provided by Del CC Advisory Council (details further on in the paper) and their own direct observations the commissioners would decide on the most important matters requiring to be probed or investigated by them;

(c) To ensure that the quality of probe or investigation commands respect from all quarters with its incisiveness, thoroughness, impartiality and professionalism;

(d) The aspects of high quality of professionalism and lack of bias would be extremely important because it would form the basis for further action to be taken by the commissioners;

(e) Every aspect that is taken up by the commissioners need not result from investigations carried out independently on behalf of Del CC. It could also be based upon direct inputs that are in the public domain and on which action that should be taken by the government or the competent authority was being delayed with a view to letting the furore so created subside. An example are the CAG reports, which when released put the spotlight on the government and its departments and agencies but seldom lead to prosecution;

(f) On a number of occasions exposures based on leaks, inside information or investigative journalism by the media puts the government in the dock, clearly highlighting the culpability of the departments and concerned individuals. In these cases further endorsement by the commissioners after due diligence to verify the correctness and authenticity of the exposure would add to the pressure on the government to take action;

(g) Once the reputation of Del CC is established and the status of commissioners begins to command respect the government would have no choice but to follow through on the reports put out by the commissioners;

(h) Even the judiciary in certain cases could take suo motu cognizance of the commission's reports;

(i) Occasionally misconduct of government departments and agencies that is seldom allowed to be probed by impartial investigating teams would come to the knowledge of commissioners through the RTI route or from whistle blowers serving within, who would very much like to report cases of corruption once they have confidence that inputs made available to the commissioners cannot be traced back to them. (The method of ensuring foolproof secrecy in this regard is spelled out later on in the paper);

(j) It is often the case that when offences committed by police personnel or corruption in government departments are highlighted in the media the culprits so named are suspended and transferred, or police persons so named are sent to the lines. The public is seldom allowed to know the follow up. The commissioners would be able to demand to be told of the follow up actions.

7. The guidelines spelled out in the preceding paragraphs for the functioning of the commissioners are not exhaustive. The list can be expanded should the commissioners choose to do so. Once the commissioners have made up their mind on the cases that require further action on their part after the reports have been received and analyzed by experts selected by them for doubly checking on their veracity, the commissioners could take any of the pathways listed below for urging follow up action by the government or the concerned competent authorities:

(a) Endorsing the reports prepared by them to the Chief Justices of the Delhi High Court or the Supreme Court so that the concerned court can take suo motu note and direct further action as deemed fit;
(b) Sending the report to the Prime Minister with copies to The President, Vice President, Lok Sabha Speaker and any other dignitary or competent authority for further action;
(c) Press briefing to the Media;
(d) Requesting the Advisory Council to hold conclaves on the issues involved for creating greater public awareness as also eliciting views from the larger body of NGOs, Lawyers' Associations, professional bodies involved with the particular subject;
(e) Should the commissioners perceive that the government were shying away from taking action on the reports or trying to cover up, the commissioners could decide to file a PIL in the Delhi High Court or the Supreme Court secure in the knowledge that the judiciary would realise that the PIL had become the last resort after all attempts to secure remedial action from the government or the concerned authorities had failed;

(f) In selected cases the commissioners might decide to forward their reports directly to the directors CBI, Enforcement Directorate, Commissioner Central Board of Direct Taxes, Chief Vigilance Commissioner, Election Commission, CIC and any other authority that the commissioners feel should pursue the matter.

Replacement and Turnover of the Commissioners

8. The first set of three commissioners having been selected (as brought out earlier in paragraph 5 above) would have a tenure of five years, so that they are in a position to stabilize the new entity being created as a model for the rest of the country as also to impart institutional vigour to it in its formative stage.

9. After the first five years or on one of the commissioners retiring prematurely for whatever reason, the procedure for selecting the replacement would be analogous to the selection of the first set of commissioners. Additionally, the retiring commissioner or commissioners' recommendations for successors would also be given due consideration by the Advisory Council. After the stepping down of the first set of commissioners all subsequent commissioners selected for Del CC would have three-year tenure, which could be extended by two years. During the transition from the first set of commissioners to their successors it would be ensured that the intake of the new commissioners and departure of the old commissioners is so arranged that there is a reasonable degree of overlap so that continuity and smooth succession is maintained. The method of staggered replacement can be decided upon separately by the Advisory Council.

DEL CC ADVISORY COUNCIL

Composition

10. The Del CC Advisory Council (hereafter referred to as AC) shall consist of fifteen members at any one time. The first AC will have the following composition:

(a) Two members each from the prime movers, i.e., Common Cause, NNFI and MRGG, preferably Trustees;

(b) One member each from other NGOs that have been associated with Common Cause, MRGG or NNFI or those who become associated with Del CC after its setting up. Once the first AC comes into being subsequent intake and rotation will be decided by this body. Members of the first AC will have tenure of five years. In the case of the prime movers (Common Cause, MRGG and NNFI) the initial members could continue for an additional period of three years. However, the endeavor during the first five years tenure of the AC should be to strengthen and streamline the procedure in such a manner that Del CC, at least at the level of the AC, does not become over-dependent upon the founding persons and younger members are gradually brought in to carry the torch forward.

Charter and Function

11. The smooth function, efficacy and prestige of the Del CC will primarily rest on the AC. Therefore, its functioning becomes as important if not more important than that of the citizen commissioners, for it would be the AC that would embody the DNA of Del CC, in a manner of speaking. Broadly the charter of the Advisory Council would include, inter alia:

(a) Be the creator, maintainer and repository of Del CC in all its dimensions;

(b) To select the Del CC commissioners and provide them secretarial support for their functioning;

(c) To maintain constant liaison with the citizen commissioners ;

(d) To uphold the charter of the citizen commissioners. However, if required to do so it could ask any of the commissioners to step down should it come to light that in the overall interest of Del CC the continuing of the said commissioner might not be in the interest of the citizens of Delhi. So that there is no heart burning should such an extreme step become necessary, the commissioners when selected and prior to their acceptance would be briefed about the particular clause. The decision to request a commissioner to step down would require the written approval of at least twelve of the AC members.

(e) Since Common Cause has an established office, the Secretary General of the AC would be provided by Common Cause, as also the use of its premises till alternative arrangements can be made;

(f) The President of the AC will alternate between Common Cause, MRGG and NNFI for the first two years rotating every four months. Subsequently, the President will be selected on six monthly basis from other associates, in turn;

(g) The deed of Del CC, which will be a registered body under the Society Act 1861 after having been duly vetted by competent attorneys, will be approved by the AC before tasking the law firm appointed for the purpose to register the deed. It would be the responsibility of the Secretary General to monitor progress;

(h) The AC would also be responsible for creating a corpus for Del CC, accepting donations and for maintaining transparency of Del CC accounts. Further details on the maintenance of accounts are given separately in the ensuing paragraphs;

(i) The Secretary General would be responsible for creating and maintaining the Del CC website;

(j) Once the corpus has been created and donations start flowing the AC will approve the staff requirement for assisting the Secretary General in the discharge of his duties.

DUTIES AND FUNCTION OF THE SECRETARY GENERAL OF THE ADVISORY COUNCIL

The guidelines for the functioning of the Secretary General are given below:

(a) For the initial period of five years the Secretary General will be provided by Common Cause. Subsequently the Secretary General can be provided by any of the associates or hired after approval by the AC;

(b) For the first two years, till the fund position improves, Common Cause would generally undertake Secretarial and other support for the Secretary General. Associates that are in a position to provide financial support for the purpose should endeavor to do so;

(c) The Secretary General would be responsible for keeping the minutes of all meetings, issuing circulars, details of associates and list of their members, maintaining accounts and all other secretarial work pertaining to Del CC. For this the AC would provide the Secretary General with the requisite number of assistants;

(d) The Secretary General would send out notices for meetings of the AC at least once every quarter after getting the dates approved by the President. Emergent meetings can be called at any time on the request of the President or the Secretary General;

(e) While it would be the endeavor to keep the website of Del CC upto date the AC after going through the minutes of the meeting will indicate to the Secretary General those aspects which could be put on the Website.

(f) The importance and criticality of the role of the Secretary General as the linchpin of the Del CC and the AC cannot be over-emphasized. Hence his selection would have to be carefully gone into by the prime movers in the first instance and the AC during subsequent changeovers.

(g) Ordinarily, the Secretary General should also be changed every five years. If the work of the incumbent is found to be unsatisfactory, the individual could be asked to demit office by a simple majority of the AC members voting at a special session held for the purpose.

FUNDING AND MAINTENANCE OF ACCOUNTS

Corpus

12. Essentially Del CC represents the coming together of concerned citizens from Delhi and from other parts of India for stemming the rot in governance that could severely undermine democratic functioning at the Centre and the States. The prime movers, AC and the citizen commissioners comprise concerned citizens who have been working since long for uplifting society and improvement of governance in Delhi and the country. The majority of them having worked selflessly for many years have acquired an appreciable degree of respect and credibility. None of them would be seeking remuneration for their efforts during the institutionalization of Del CC or its continued functioning thereafter. If anything they would be contributors. Nevertheless, the scope of the task that is envisaged and the supporting staff of dedicated and competent persons who would have to be paid decent salaries would require a continuous flow of a minimum level of funds so that the work of Del CC is not hampered due to lack of funds.

13. While it may not be possible at this point in time to assign a figure for the corpus it should be the endeavor of the prime movers and their supporters and associates to mobilize donations so that an initial figure of 2.5 crore rupees is available for the corpus. Subsequently, it could be built up to 5 crores. For achieving this figure the charter of Del CC

will be proclaimed to the public through various channels and support groups. The prime movers will also hold public meetings and explain the charter at institutions like India International Centre, India Habitat Centre, Delhi Gymkhana Club, Chelmsford Club, Press Club, CII, FICCI, ASSOCHAM, PHHDCCI and other selected forums.

Maintenance of Accounts

14. Prior to collection or acceptance of any sum it would be ensured by the AC that the trust fund, duly registered with any of the public sector banks is first set up so that all monies received are directly deposited in the Del CC account. Once the account has been set up AC members would send out letters asking for donations to various bodies and individuals who they feel would be able to donate towards setting up the corpus or in the form of monthly or yearly donations for the running of Del CC. At a later stage tamper proof collection boxes would be set up for Del CC collections at appropriate places. A methodology would be worked out for visiting these boxes on a weekly basis by a team of three members or office holders designated by AC for the purpose.

15. The Accounts Cell that would be responsible for collection of donations and maintenance of accounts would function under the aegis of the Secretary General. The Accounts Cell would comprise a treasurer and two assistant treasurers. The accounts would be updated on a daily basis on all working days. On a weekly basis these would be approved by the Secretary General; The President of the AC would inspect the accounts in the first week of each month. The updated accounts would be put on the website of Del CC. Expenditure guidelines and instructions for authorization of signing of cheques jointly by the Secretary General and a nominated treasurer will be laid down in a separate instruction after consultation with the chartered accountants appointed by the AC.

RTI AND WHISTLEBLOWERS

16. The AC and citizen commissioners would normally get their inputs for looking into areas that require further investigation by the latter from the media, published documents, CAG and other reports on which the government had not acted. Further source would be through the medium of RTI and whistle blowers.

RTI

17. RTI can be utilized for seeking information in various ways. One way would be for the AC to initiate RTI directly on behalf of Del CC by nominating any of the staff members to do the filing. Further, an appeal would go out to the citizens of Delhi and NGOs and associates to share RTI inputs extracted by them with the AC, wherever the RTI in question dealt with larger public issues and not inputs sought in personal cases. Thereafter, it would be for the AC to decide upon follow up action.

Whistleblowers

18. As in the case of RTI an appeal would go out to the public that whistleblowers in the know of corruption, malfeasance, misfeasance, defalcation and other illegal activities in government departments and agencies could write confidentially to the citizen commissioners by name giving details of the misconduct, misdeed, commission or omission that would require to be investigated by non-partisan and non-subverted entities.

19. The methodology of assuring foolproof protection of identity to the whistleblower would be made known through the Del CC website and through media channels. The procedure followed would be that any letter addressed to the citizen commissioners at the Del CC address would straightaway be put into the safe deposit box after registration of all incoming mail. All such sealed envelopes would be opened jointly by the commissioners at Del CC main

office on a fortnightly or monthly basis as decided by the Secretary General in consultation with the commissioners. The commissioners after opening and inspecting all such letters would enter the name of the whistleblower, letter number and date and one or two line synopsis of the aspect divulged in a register kept in the safe deposit box for the purpose. Similarly, the letter would also be returned to the safe deposit. The commissioners would then decide upon the follow up action to be taken. They would also apprise the AC on the intended follow up action without divulging the name of the whistleblower. In this fashion once confidence of the public is gained that Del CC has a failsafe methodology for protection of identity of the whistleblower many illegalities, cases of corruption and even cases of officials indulging in anti-national activities would keep flowing to the Del CC.

20. It is not necessary at this stage to put down guidelines for the follow up action to be taken by citizen commissioners. They would exercise their judgment on how to proceed with cases that require further action and the priority to be allocated to each case.

PUBLIC SUPPORT

21. NGOs that have built up a sound reputation of working in this domain over the years can count on support of several lawyers, professionals, serving and retired diplomats and bureaucrats, senior citizens, youth groups, social service groups and other categories of persons for affording assistance for all good causes. Once the credentials of Del CC have been established all such support and affiliation available to the NGOs would automatically be available to Del CC. This support becomes invaluable because respected lawyers, professionals, journalists and other members of the public in a position to help would provide their expertise and services freely. Thus should an investigation be required to be carried out for the costing, technical feasibility, quality of construction of any project, reputed architects and engineers would be co-opted by the

AC for carrying out the task and making an independent report. The same applies for any other investigation that the AC or the citizen commissioners may decide to pursue.

22. Once the results of the investigations have been evaluated by the AC and the separate independent body of experts, the AC and commissioners would decide upon the next steps. The next steps could include, inter alia:

(a) Briefing the President and Vice President of India where it is felt that the government at the highest level were itself suspect in the matter;

(b) Depending on the sensitivity of the case, informing the Prime Minister or the CVC and heads of the investigative agencies concerned about the matter;

(c) Going public with the investigation report ;

(d) If the government is suspect, initiate investigation to the extent possible through retired experts who had in-depth knowledge of these matters while in service;

(e) In very sensitive cases sending the report by name under a sealed cover to the chief justice of the supreme court or chief justice of the Delhi high court as the case may be ;

(f) Filing PIL on behalf of Del CC;

(g) Filing FIR in cases where it were felt that the authorities are stonewalling the case.

MISCELLANOUS ASPECTS

23. At the present juncture the charter for the Delhi Citizen Commission is being initiated by the three prime mover NGOs, namely, Common Cause, NNFI-National Network for India and MRGG- Movement for Restoration of Good Government. Before going ahead with this mission the prime movers have held several discussions amongst themselves and many associates in Delhi and other parts of the country who have been getting together from time to time to bring about improvement in governance and the

deteriorating law and order in the country. The Del CC charter after it is approved by all concerned and institutionalized in Delhi could serve as a model for all states and cities where citizen groups could come forward to establish their own charters. The prime movers and the Advisory Council of Del CC, once Del CC starts functioning, would be available for assistance and advice for similar efforts elsewhere in the country.

24. The target date for commencement of operations by Del CC after registration is 1st April, 2013.

ANNEXURES

[Comprising MRGG petitions to the Judiciary, Missives to Decision-Makers and Articles that Underpin and Supplement the formulations in Chapters 1 to 10]

INDIAN DEMOCRACY HAS REACHED A HISTORIC TURNING POINT

Your vote may still allow India to keep its tryst with destiny. Destiny has not forsaken India. We failed to keep the tryst. It still beckons. Do not again fail your country. Do not put your destiny, and that of your country, in rotten hands. There must be better people to lead the nation. People who India can be proud of. People who can hold their head high. Your vote can make the vital difference. Do not be swayed by the purveyors of hatred and division. The nation has had enough of Muslim voters, Hindu voter and other such voters. It now waits for the Indian voter. It waits for you.

AN APPEAL TO THE PM

This is a follow up to earlier letters on the subject as Convenor, MRGG. It must have come to your notice that in the course of the last few days the CISF personnel at the IGIA in Delhi have caught several people working at the airport in various misdemeanors, including pilferage and overcharging of alighting passengers. As reported, in almost all cases, the offenders have been let off with a warning or a small fine. IGIA is the nation's showpiece. If this is the state of affairs in the capital city under the aegis of agencies directly under the central government you can imagine as to what the state of discipline might be elsewhere in the country.

In the light of the foregoing may I be permitted to recommend the following actions:

- The heads of all central authorities/agencies (in the present case the Airport Authority of India) should be warned that if they are unable to enforce discipline they have no business to be holding that charge.
- Unless exemplary punishment is meted out, at least where visibility is highest for the rest of the country, the decline in standards will continue.
- Names of persons caught in such acts should be automatically circulated to all agencies of the central and state governments so that they are unable to spread the rot elsewhere. Even non-government agencies should be able to access such websites before offering employment.

Over the years we have watched with dismay the lowering of standards in most fields where the government is directly concerned. Because of this lack disciplinary standards are being lowered in many of the uniformed organizations as well. You may like to intervene.

Hon'ble Dr. Manmohan Singh
Prime Minister

GHETTOISATION OF THE POLITICAL ELITE

Enclosed please find a copy of the article **Onset of Terminal Degeneracy: Ghetto-isation of the Political Elite,** prior to its publication. While the article is self-explanatory I wish to highlight the point that since we are passing through a turbulent phase of our democracy some tough measures will have to be taken to right matters in spheres where **terminal degeneracy** has set in. When cancer becomes widespread it is either rooted out completely or it destroys the body. Where firmness is called for half-hearted measures engender a false sense of well-being.

Nobody would want the judiciary to go beyond a given point if other alternatives were available. It is because we have run out of softer options that the public whole-heartedly and overwhelmingly supports what is being referred to, for want of a more appropriate term, as "judicial activism"

A simple analogy will illustrate the point. In the high seas if a boat springs a leak and starts listing the weight has to be re-distributed to prevent the boat from capsizing; till the leak has been plugged. In like fashion, when the body politic demonstrates its ability to steer a steady course judicial activism will automatically wane. When that moment comes the judiciary will revert to the **benign overwatch** mode.

Mr. Justice J S Verma
Supreme Court of India
Tilak Marg
New Delhi-110001.

POLITY AND GOVERNANCE

26 February 1997

This refers to two articles **Spread of Anarchy: is the state Acquiescing** and **Proliferation of the Bihar Model of Governance** well before they were published. Two days ago the country was amazed by your statement in Parliament. Sadly, what you said was true. You are the first Home Minister to have admitted in public that the state of affairs in UP (and perhaps elsewhere as well) was verging on the anarchic. This, in itself, is an important first step i.e. acknowledging that all is not well. I would now like to make a recommendation for the second step, for stemming the rot.

It is suggested that a new committee be set up under Shri N N Vohra to recommend steps for dismantling the politico-criminal nexus. With Shri Vohra the other committee members could be Shri Ved Marwaha and one or two persons of eminence, competence and integrity. The Second Vohra Committee would be given one hundred days to make their recommendations. The recommendations would be divided into two categories. The first category would comprise those recommendations which could be implemented straightaway under the aegis of the Home Minister or the Cabinet. The second category would consist of steps that require judicial or legislative sanction before implementation.

The Committee after presenting its recommendations would have the **mandate to implement these on the ground,** in concert with the concerned ministries and departments. A special dispensation to this effect should be incorporated in the charter of the Committee at inception. The time frame for implementing the category one recommendations should also be laid down. It is possible for the Home Minister to *suo motu* announce the setting up of the Second Vohra Committee. Before that, however, the Speaker of the Lok Sabha and a few other respected leaders or legislators can be taken into confidence. **The public support for such a move would be overwhelming.** At a later stage, or concomitantly, another committee to re-vitalise the functioning of the premier intelligence and investigative agencies should also be set up. The national interest must be safeguarded here and now at all cost, at any cost. Those who oppose such a move must be deemed to be anti-national. There is no other way of looking at it.

There is no time to lose. Please seize the initiative.

Shri Indrajit Gupta
Home Minister
Ministry of Home Affairs
North Block; New Delhi-110001

AGENDA FOR A CITIZEN-CENTRIC GOVERNMENT

A summary of the national agenda, which will guide the MRGG in the selection (or backing) of candidates is given below:

- Promotion of effective governance at all levels by excluding political interference in the day-to-day work of the civil services and law and order forces.
- Upholding the principal of accountability at all levels of governance.
- Support of public action litigation by concerned citizens' action groups.
- Supporting special legislation for the removal and prosecution of corrupt ministers.
- Strengthening the agencies for effective monitoring and protection of the environment.
- Eschewing caste-based politics and communalism in any form by upholding the spirit of the Constitution.
- Greater transparency in the government's functioning in areas not directly related to national defence and state security.
- Security of tenure of civil servants.
- Transparent procedures for the selection of the most competent persons (not necessarily bureaucrats) to head government enterprises and undertakings.
- The setting up of independent commissions for effecting transfers in the police and other enforcement agencies in line with the Police Commission report.
- Population stabilisation as an overriding national priority.

- Strengthening SAARC.
- Evolving a national consensus on vital issues related to India's long term security interests.
- Setting up of properly constituted National Security Council.
- Creation of ombudsman.

The mission of Resurgent India Movement (RIM) in its simplest form is the 'Revitalisation of India'.

AN APPEAL FOR DEALING WITH ENCROACHMENTS

1. Your Lordship hardly needs to be apprised of the menace of encroachments on to footpaths that, in turn, force pedestrians on to the roads, resulting in accidents whose number keeps increasing with each passing year. The Courts have been intervening in this regard on account of PILs, *suo motu* interventions based on reports, or for any other reason. In a system that is tending towards terminal degeneration, the Courts have willy-nilly become the last repository of hope for the public. Close on the heels of the demolitions undertaken in Lajpat Nagar (and elsewhere in Delhi) is a press report along with photograph appearing in *The Indian Express,* dated April 24, 2002 (copy attached) citing a brazen example of disregard for the public welfare on the part of a legislator.

2. It is felt that the time may have come for the Courts to issue a set of general warnings/guidelines/instructions so that such violations, that have no business to be taking place in the first instance, are automatically dealt with without going through the cumbersome procedure of Public Interest Litigation or Court intervention. In this regard, we recommend the following actions for consideration by the Honourable Court:

(a) Directions to all the concerned authorities that in cases of accidents taking place on the road where a pedestrian or pedestrians could be deemed to have moved on to the road due to the impediment created by the encroachment, the party or individual that carried out the encroachment would be liable to: (i) Bear all costs for medical expenses of the injured party; (ii) In case of death the payment of a sum of Rs.10 lakhs to the next of kin/dependant of the deceased; (iii) A fine of Rs.10 lakhs to be deposited into the public treasury for nuisance/harassment/ inconvenience caused to the public at large; (iv) All such fines levied from the encroacher would be over and above the solatium or other reliefs admissible to the injured/deceased party under the existing regulations on the subject.

(b) Automatic procedure for citizens to report such encroachments/harassment/public nuisance/inconvenience caused under registered cover, giving details to a 'designated authority'. The designated authority would thereafter be obliged to take the following actions within seven working days of receipt of complaint: (i) Send acknowledgement in writing to the person sending the complaint under registered cover. (The newspapers could also be advised to follow the same procedure); (ii) The designated authority would be obliged to order (automatically) the removal of the encroachment at the earliest, but not later than 30 days after having received the intimation of the encroachment; no stay would be allowed in cases of encroachments that are obviously a case of land grabbing or falling into certain categories that do not admit of doubt about the illegality of the encroachment; (iii) Automatic issuance of show cause notices for termination of services to functionaries, whose duty it was in the first instance to see to it that encroachments did not take place in the areas falling under their jurisdiction; (iv) Similar action against the SHO of the police station in cases where encroachment was so conspicuous that it could not have escaped detection; and where it was clearly the duty of the concerned police authority to take appropriate action; (v) Follow up action by the (concerned) heads of departments of the functionaries on whom the show cause notice had been served to be reported back in writing to the designated authority; (vi) The designated authority to automatically paste all complaints with dates received, action taken and follow up reports on a website.

Details of the website should be made known to the public.

3. The aim of the recommendations made above - which can be suitably modified for a given situation - is to streamline the procedure for removal of encroachments. The public at large should be able to expect remedial action as a matter of right from functionaries paid with taxpayer's monies so that ordinary people can get on with their lives without being forced to go through lengthy redress procedures or court interventions. Where a department, or its functionary, is unable to discharge the laid down responsibilities it should be possible for the public to demand that the department be wound up or the functionary concerned discharged after suitable disciplinary action and the function be handed over to another body or nongovernmental organization for a trial period till a better alternative is established. Any other suitable arrangement could also be considered. Since Delhi is the capital of India the coming into force of simple procedures that reduce harassment/undue inconvenience to the public could serve as model for the rest of the country.

Hon'ble Justice S.B. Sinha
Chief Justice
Delhi High Court
Sher Shah Suri Marg, New Delhi - 110 001

29 April, 2002

MISSIVE TO PARTY LEADERS

For several weeks there has been trenchant criticism of the manner in which the unrest in Gujarat has been handled. Your party has been in the vanguard of this criticism. Justifiably so, because no administration worth its salt should accept the continuing carnage long after any justification for a spontaneous outburst - following the Godhra incident-can be tenable. Regardless of who is to blame, it is clearly a national tragedy. In a manner of speaking all of us must share the blame for the gradual degeneration of governance that has been taking place in India, irrespective of the political dispensation in control, whether in the States or at the Centre. Governance cannot come to such a sorry pass unless the process had been allowed to decay over a long period of time. Since concerned citizens of this country bemoan the shredding of communal harmony, your party must take the lead in reassuring the public that its concern is real and that it is not out to obtain political mileage from the tragedy. Throughout the refrain has been that there has been a breakdown of law and order. Law and order is a state subject except where central intervention is necessitated under Articles 355 and 356 of the Constitution. Therefore, the Congress Party can prove its sincerity by announcing that it is undertaking without delay the reforms set out in the Police Commission report. Most experts, and well-wishers of the country, agree that the Report constituted an outstanding reform effort. Please make an unambiguous declaration that the Party intends to incorporate the most important recommendations relating to the selection of the head of the State Police and the transfer of police personnel. Give a clear time frame for the implementation of the reforms.

Should you take action as recommended above not only will the top political leadership set a fine example of far-reaching national import, but it would have sent out a message that the Congress Party means business. In that case, MRGG and like-minded people across the length and breadth of the country would be happy to lend support. Additionally, it would have an electrifying effect on the nation, cutting across party lines. The opportunity to prove your Party's *bona fides* is at hand. Please grasp it.

Dr. Manmohan Singh
Shri Shivraj Patil
Ms. Sonia Gandhi

6 May, 2002

MARCH TO FOLLY

This is a personal letter. As a minister in the government that is running the country I seriously recommend that you obtain a copy of the book *March to Folly* by Barbara Tuchman. It cites interesting examples from the Athens and Sparta discord up to the modern times to show how people at the helm of affairs refuse to heed the warning signs. In every case mentioned in the book the signs were all there, unmistakable, for the people at the top to have taken note and make the necessary corrections to their policies. The BJP, presently, is in the same category. It has to break away from the extreme right elements in the party and lean more towards the Centre. It is losing support faster than you think. From time immemorial the Hindu mind - although the term Hindu did not exist then - was synonymous with subtlety. The blunderbus approach simply will not work.

I am writing in the hope that good sense prevails. All is not yet lost. Much can be regained by concentrating on good governance and positive action.

Shri Jaswant Singh
Foreign Minister 8 May, 2002

REFORMING THE POLICE

I am enclosing copy of letter dated April 29, 2002 sent to central Congress leaders, including Smt. Sonia Gandhi, on the need for reforms recommended by the Police Commission in their report. Similar action had been taken several years earlier when the late Shri Indrajit Gupta was the Home Minister. He had lamented that he had written to the Chief Ministers to undertake these reforms, which he had strongly recommended, for adoption. In a newspaper interview he gave out that none of the Chief Ministers had even replied to his letter. I had written back to him to ascertain as to what had prevented him from incorporating the reforms in Delhi Police since the Lieutenant Governor of Delhi was directly answerable to the MHA. I did not get any reply.

I have been following your career as a politician over the years. You have shown exemplary courage and 'uprightness' over a long period of time. My belief is shared by many others with whom I have interacted. Can we request you to take the first step towards the restoration of law and order in the country by undertaking these reforms in Kerala. If not outright, in one step, at least incrementally, over a three year period. You might just turn out to be the catalyst for national reconstruction in this regard. You must have noticed that politicians of every hue condemned the happenings in Gujarat. Not one of them advocated the type of reforms that could obviate the recurrence of such nightmarish situation in the future.

Hon'ble Shri A.K. Antony
Chief Minister of Kerala
Secretariat
Trivandrum - 1 (Kerala) 29 July, 2003

LETTER TO L.K. ADVANI

As Convenor MRGG [Movement for Restoration of Good Governance] I must express my dismay at the actions being taken by the government at the Center in respect of the New Master Plan. I would have thought that senior political leaders by now would have comprehended that the public having shed its gullibility a long time back are not fools. They see through the election gimmicks. Otherwise, Prakash Singh Badal would have gained an absolute majority in the last assembly elections in Punjab. The concessions made by him were so blatantly election-oriented and so patently against the long-term interests of the State that even his staunchest allies were aghast. It is for the same reason that many governments in Europe that brought in blatantly populist measures failed to retain their majorities.

What is even more inexplicable in the present case on the part of senior leaders backing the initiative is their complete *lack of feeling* for the city, which has been their home for decades on end, irrespective of their former provenance. Their children have grown up in Delhi; they themselves have blossomed into national leaders from here. And yet for illusory, short-sighted election gains they are ready to sacrifice the well being of one of India's most beautiful cities - the capital of so many dynasties that ruled India. In the earlier cases even though the rulers were not truly of Indian origin they tried, almost all of them, to beautify and preserve the city. Not so the present rulers of the nation.

It is a crying shame. If this is the response of the leading politicians of the day to the city that nurtured them, what should be expected of them at the national level? It is still not too late. I appeal to you to have the government retrace its steps, in the most graceful way possible, without necessarily indicating that an about turn has taken place.

Hon'ble Shri L.K. Advani
Deputy Prime Minister

May 31, 2004

SOMNATH THE SPEAKER

Let me begin by congratulating you on your election as the Speaker of the14th Lok Sabha. I had the pleasure of meeting you only once. You might recall that immediately following the Gujarat carnage Shri S K Singh, the former foreign secretary had convened a meeting in the India International Centre, Committee Room. Others present included N.N. Vohra, Naresh Chandra, Harish Khare, Zoya Hassan and perhaps one or two others. I think you had chaired that meeting.

After retirement in January 1995 I proposed a model for the restoration of good governance at the India International Centre in October 1995. Lo and behold, the model became a movement for restoration of good government, the acronym MRGG remaining the same. (Incidentally, the model was translated into several languages, being a universal model amenable to modification). The UN Secretary General had it circulated in the UN, as did the European Commission to its departments in Brussels. I became its Convenor and in that capacity sent out the *MRGG Appeal to the Parliamentarians of the Thirteenth Lok Sabha* in 1999. I do not think it had any worthwhile effect. It was business as usual in a very short while. I submit to you that the MRGG appeal holds good for the 14th Lok Sabha as well. Perhaps it can be translated into Hindi as well and circulated to the new members under your aegis.

I would like to end by wishing you all success in the onerous duty that you have accepted. I believe that the good wishes of all our countrymen who know of your past contributions to the polity are with you.

Mr. Somnath Chatterjee
Speaker
Lok Sabha Secretariat 29 October, 2004

AN ALERT TO PRESIDENT KALAM

In recent months I had delivered talks at IIT, Kharagpur and BITS, Pilani. At both these institutes I met the directors and faculty heads. Earlier, I had also met the department heads at CBRI in Roorkee. From these interactions I was dismayed to learn that not many people were opting for the 'civil engineering' stream. The few who do join, albeit reluctantly, are generally the ones at the lowest rungs of the intake. If this trend is not righted the country is likely to face a major disaster, what with large infrastructure projects coming up in a big way and not many qualified civil engineers being around to effectively monitor the quality of the projects. The same applies to the field of agriculture. Here again there are few takers. Besides bemoaning the fact that electronics, mechanical engineering and computer related programmes were attracting the vast majority of the students, the department heads were at a loss as to the remedial measures to be taken.

I am writing to you because of your known concerns in the field of education. You would be in a position to suggest remedial measures to the government and the concerned institutions in order to restore a semblance of balance so that infrastructure and agricultural development do not get neglected in the coming years.

Dr. APJ Abdul Kalam
President of India

25 January, 2005

COURT NOTICE TO ATTORNEY GENERAL ON PLEA FOR 'NEGATIVE VOTE'

I am writing in connection with the notice issued by the Supreme Court to the Attorney General on a petition seeking a right for the voter to cast a "negative vote" in an election by choosing the "none of the candidates" option in the electronic voting machine (EVM).

As convener Movement for Restoration of Good Government (MRGG) I have been closely involved with several issues relating to electoral reforms and have a different opinion on this matter, which I am now putting before your Lordship for consideration. I believe that the negative vote incorporation could stir a hornet's nest. My reasons are spelled out in the ensuing paragraphs.

The negative vote or 'none of the above' feature could be used by communal groups to vitiate the electoral process. For example, a religious leader in a given constituency might issue *a fatwa* for the casting of a negative vote unless candidates were put up from a particular denomination. Just one example has been given. There are others.

It is also worth considering as to how many voters possess any real knowledge about the numerous candidates whose names appear on the list when they go and exercise their vote. Even some of the well read amongst them would not have information about *all* the candidates, many of whose names are put up at the last moment. The time is simply not enough for the average voter to inform himself/herself about the background and potential of all the candidates.

I believe this issue has far-reaching ramifications that have not been fully explored by all concerned.

Mr. Justice R.C. Lahoti,
Chief Justice; Supreme Court

February 21, 2005

JUDICIAL ACTIVISIM

Inducing Judicial Activism (or Having Their Cake and Eating it Too)

"Justice being taken away, what is State, but a band of robbers". St. Augustine

Of late there has been a fair amount of debate on 'Judicial Activism', some of it informed, much of it less well informed. Judicial Activism should not be looked at in standalone fashion. It has to be viewed against the backdrop of the vertiginous decline in the probity and conduct of the political class across the political spectrum - at the Centre as well as in the States. In fact, if one were to take a sounding as to which class the people of India dislike the most, it would hardly come as a surprise if the political class were to emerge as the most despised lot. That the judiciary itself has lost much of its lustre can hardly be cause for comfort for those looking up to the Courts.

Attention is first of all invited to excerpts from a talk given on 2nd August 2006 to a distinguished audience on a theme relating to national security, good governance, jurisprudence and allied aspects:

"Therefore, if one takes the line of thinking opened up by the Honorable Supreme Court to its logical conclusion one comes up with the dreadful deduction that today the biggest threat to the security of India might be the political class, full 20 percent of whose members happen to have criminal cases registered against them. If the percentage as given out by the Election Commission is right then the criminal class that has entered Parliament is perhaps one of the single largest blocks, although affiliated to political parties across the political divide.

Leaving the rest of the country to fend for itself the political class cocoons itself in the security provided by gun-toting bodyguards paid for by the exchequer, irrespective of whether the persons so protected have a number of murder, dacoity or rape cases pending against them. .... In all other countries the political class comes together in the face of national emergencies. In India they come together to undermine the decisions of the highest judicial bodies in the country. In no other country in the world are the decisions of the Supreme Court - the final arbiter - overturned or thwarted as summarily as is presently happening in India".

It is against this background that the debate on judicial activism should be entered. A distinguished (former) governor of the Reserve Bank of India had opined that it had been his experience that a large number of decisions at the highest levels of governance had not been taken in the national interest, but in the interests of the political parties, vested interests, or other such considerations (that did not augur well for the country). (Unquote)

The abysmal lot of a large percentage of India's population is there for all to see. Looking at India's future in the face of the fast emerging global threats, what has the government done to meet these challenges? A few well-documented and incontrovertible examples highlight the national decline. The Government of India and the state governments have demonstrated their complete inability to save the flora and fauna of India - the forests are being decimated at an increasing rate; they have been poached routinely for over 50 years. In spite of spending thousands of crores of rupees the pollution levels in the Ganga and the Yamuna might actually have gone up. These two rivers systems are famous for a variety of reasons. Should similar surveys be undertaken for many other waterways and water bodies the state of decline would be seen to be far worse. If left to the political class the national capital would be in shambles in less than a decade. One can go on in this vein indefinitely to show that laws are being flouted with greater and greater impunity, mostly by the legislators and people at the helm of affairs. Law and order as understood in civilized society has virtually disappeared for the common man. As if the burdens of the *aam admi* were not already beyond his capacity to bear the politicians add to his woes by repeated *bandhs* that are a nightmare for the daily wage earner. Equality before the law is more in the breach than in practice. And yet the state governments who are the biggest offenders in this regard appear to be showing extreme reluctance to usher in the changes in police functioning as directed by the Supreme Court. It is incomprehensible that full 60 years after Independence the Government of India has not yet thought fit to amend the Police Act, a relic of the colonial regime that dates back to 1861.

Judicial Intervention

In this sea of dreariness and despair the higher judiciary has held out some hope for the people of India. If terminal decline has been arrested in certain areas of governance it is due to the yeoman service provided by the higher judiciary - in spite of glaring lapses in the past - and the Election Commission of India. They remain beacons of hope for India; and for many other countries that have started looking towards India. There should be no doubt in the mind of the political class that the public at large overwhelmingly supports most of the judicial interventions undertaken in recent years at the highest levels. It is certainly not in the long-term interest of Indian democracy that the judiciary be brought into ridicule by all and sundry, especially the political class.

Many of the political actions and decisions fall so patently foul of the tenets of the Constitution or the working of the constitution even under the degraded norms now prevalent in the running of the government that the courts have no choice but to step in. A few examples will suffice:

- A chief minister of a state decides to give land rights to tribals without waiting for notification of the revised bill by the government at the centre. Needless to say that over and above the fact that the rules have yet to be communicated, the said legislation might itself be challenged in the highest court;
- Enactment by state governments of reservations on the basis of religion in clear contravention of the framework of the constitution in this regard.

Other examples can be cited where political parties when in power go ahead with outrageous enactments, or promises of enactments if voted to power, knowing full well that the courts would have no choice but to strike them down. In all such cases the political leadership unmindful of the long-term consequences of their decisions for coming generations or the national interest *do so in full knowledge* of the illegality or non-maintainability of their actions; being clear in their minds that the courts would strike them down. Vote bank politics at the cost of the national interest and, at times, the ecological well-being of coming generations is fast becoming the rule rather than the exception. By indulging in malpractices of this nature the political parties have found the way *to eating their cake and having it too.* By these means they not only provoke the courts to become judicially active to safeguard the constitution or the interest of the country as a whole, the politicians go a step further and denigrate the judicial intervention so induced; and thereby pretend to show themselves to be the champions of the narrow interests whom they wish to appease, placate, or simply to perpetuate their vote banks. Slowly, but surely, the governments (at the Centre and the States) are divesting themselves of the capacity to govern, thus forcing the judiciary to take up the slack in the face of the formers' pusillanimity or partisanship.

The political class should sit back and take another look inwards, while they have the freedom to do so. By ganging up to undermine the judiciary they are on a path beset with great dangers. It is because of the benignity of the judiciary while dealing with cases of politicians at the highest levels that they continue to enjoy their freedom and ill-gotten gains. Should they willfully shake the edifice they could end up being the worst sufferers.

Hon'ble Mr. Justice S.H. Kapadia
Chief Justice; Supreme Court,

April 25, 2011

(Copy of article published earlier)

PLEA TO OPPOSITION LEADER L.K. ADVANI

I am enclosing copy of letter dated 7 January 2009 to the Prime Minister. I would like to make the same appeal to you on this matter. Regardless of who forms the next government, unless the two major national parties act in unison on some of the graver aspects that threaten to destroy the fabric of democracy in India, both of them would have lost the golden opportunity to set things right. Conceivably it might be the last time for years to come before they are able to regain their stature and position.

After the fading away of Vajpayee ji you remain the elder statesman of the two national parties. You must take it upon yourself to interact with the Prime Minister to jointly ward off this threat to the future of Indian democracy as you did after 26/11 for ushering in the bill to create the National Investigation Authority (NIA).

Hon'ble Shri L.K. Advani

DEGENERATION OF THE POLITICAL CLASS

(Mail to the CEC)

It is time to fairly and squarely confront the question posed in the subject heading without further delay. A stage has been reached where there is scant doubt in the minds of the general public that the national interest and, more importantly, national security are being undermined in the interest of vote bank politics, political compulsions of coalition governments and even downright political skullduggery. None of the parties are above this downslide. A point has now been reached where instead of being apologetic or shame-faced, political leaders brazenly justify their actions by blaming the opposition for having carried out similar acts whilst in government. While the rest of the world endeavours to go in for 'best practices', the Indian Political Class, almost without exception, benchmarks its actions against 'worst practices'. That national interest and, lately, even national security are being undermined for short-sighted, short-term political gains is now a given. Very few people in India doubt this. The question before the country is as to how far the Election Commission, the Judiciary, responsible government officials and the Citizens of India will continue to acquiesce in activities that are clearly assuming an anti-national hue.

As an illustration, the freedom enjoyed by Mr. Shahabuddin, the MP from Siwan in Bihar with 42 charges against him could be a case in point. As if the earlier charges against the hon'ble MP were not enough, raids carried out recently reportedly revealed the possession of illegal weapons, including automatic weapons and Night Vision Device (NVD). Almost everybody from the defense or intelligence fraternities would confirm that a NVD is not easy to come by. To individuals these are normally provided by intelligence agencies of countries that are up to no good. It should not require much guesswork to appreciate how the NVD in question might have come into the possession of the concerned individual. In any other country federal agents would have been swarming over the entire area in minutes and hours. Not so in India. In this particular case, the Governor probably had other priorities. So possibly had the Centre that appointed him. Where does one go from here?

First of all, there is a need to take the worst practices hypothesis to its logical conclusion. A chief minister of a state who was obliged to demit office on account of the charges against him has, without any qualms, subsequently been given charge of one of the most important ministries in the central government, which he could with impunity use to influence the forthcoming elections in his state. The justification given being that there was no legal bar against it and that the previous government had indulged in similar practices. The question then arises as to why Mr. Shahabuddin - an elected MP with 42 cases against him, prior to the discovery of sophisticated weaponry from questionable sources - cannot be made the Home Minister, Defense Minister, or even the Prime Minister, since the worst case hypothesis holds that there would be no legal bar against it.

It is possible to go on in this vein to show that unless the CEC and the Judiciary *suo motu* take steps to intervene directly and decisively on behalf of the public interest, which in this case coheres with the security of India, the country may yet live to rue inaction. To begin with, it is recommended that the CEC takes action to ensure that the present dispensation in Bihar is firmly kept away from the election process, which should be controlled directly by the CEC or by neutral advisors appointed directly under a judicial mandate. Meanwhile, a reference could be made to the Supreme Court to review the entire process of tainted individuals holding office as the political class might already have come under the sway of criminal elements, who might be in a position to blackmail high ranking functionaries and political leaders. The matter has to be attended to with dispatch. There is no time to lose.

Mr. B.B. Tandon
Chief Election Commissioner

WHY EMINENT PERSONS SHUT OUT FROM AUGUST OFFICES

Making of the President – But not at the cost of Unmaking of the Indian Constitution. The article reproduced below appeared in the *Economic Times* (30 May 1997), almost exactly ten years ago, prior to the election of the president of India at that time. If anything, it is more relevant today when partisan politics and vote banks politics threaten to further erode the functioning of the Constitution. In recent years it has been proved time and again that the political class on entering the hallowed sanctums of the Indian parliament in New Delhi and the State legislatures does not respect the *vox populi*. Since results are based on the constitutional lacuna of first-past-the-post the majority of the legislators are elected with very low percentages of the popular vote. By extension it implies that over 60 or 70 and, at times, even 80 to 90 percent of the constituents did not vote for the elected representative. Now almost 30 percent of them have criminal cases against them, often charged with heinous crimes, including murder, rape and dacoity. Yet the political class has neither shown the inclination nor mustered the will to further amend The Representation of People Act. Hereafter, things are likely to go from bad to worse, going by present trends.

Under these circumstances the selection of the President in July 2007 is an important landmark. The way the political parties are going about it, they appear to be bent upon politicizing the highest office in the land. Before they end up by degrading it to their own level the Indian public or "We the People" must intervene to prevent such an outcome. Almost any sounding taken from the people in practically every part of India will indicate that other than the present incumbent, Dr. APJ Abdul Kalam, none of the names being thrown up by the political class have any appeal for the people of India. Irrespective of which agency conducts the poll the candidates being suggested by the political parties would garner support of less than 9 percent as the first choice of the people, going down to as low as 1 to 3 percent.

As opposed to this India has thrown up non-political, iconic figures who are not only role models but enjoy respect even across India's frontiers. There are many such names. They include Sreedharan of Delhi Metro fame, Ratan Tata, Azim Premji of Wipro and Narayan Murthy of Infosys. Were a national referendum to be taken each one of them would easily garner well over 50 percent of the national vote. The figure could actually go up to 70 or 80 percent. The question then arises that if India is blessed with people of such high distinction, moral fiber, public esteem, proven competence in their chosen fields, enjoying international respect then why are the people of India deprived of their services for occupation of the highest office in the land. It is time that 'we the people' took the process away from a handful of political *bahubalis* and coteries and made it a truly democratic one. There is still time to do so. To achieve the desired results and to prevent political chicanery from vitiating democracy at the apex the following action needs to be started immediately by all concerned:

- Media to start highlighting the possibilities open to the public through public pressure on each one of the legislators having an electoral college vote;
- Flooding the print media with letters to the editor;
- Indicating their preferences to the electronic media every day at every opportunity;
- NGOs, RWAs, Ex-servicemen Leagues, schools, colleges, IIMs, IITs and all other bodies and institutes of similar nature to hold public meetings and pass resolutions;

- Eminent citizens' groups to personally approach and persuade some of the respected names mentioned earlier to enter themselves as candidates of peoples choice; fine tuning for ultimately putting one of them as the people's candidate would follow; CII, FICCI, ASSOCHAM and regional chambers of commerce to take the lead in this exercise;
- Any other activity of this nature that creates an irreversible momentum for democratic fulfillment.

Evidently, the people have no direct voting rights. However, since the voting by the electoral college is by secret ballot enough pressure can be put on every legislator, irrespective of the person's political leanings or hue, to exercise a conscience vote in keeping with the aspirations of the people. Should the citizens of India put their collective shoulder to this exercise for the next 6 to 8 weeks on a daily basis Indian democracy could be put back on a very sound footing. 'We the People' would have truly carried the day.

THE MAKING OF THE PRESIDENT

If, in spite of constant buffeting, the edifice of democracy still holds in India it is because some pillars of it are still strong.

Hence, whatever the means adopted to stem the rot in the body politic, it has to be ensured that the pillars that provide it some foundational stability are not weakened further. The office of the President falls into this category.

There should be no room for complacency in the era of coalition governments and fractured polities. If the spirit of the Constitution has to be safeguarded the role of the first citizen will become more crucial in the years ahead.

Hence, it behoves the polity, the public and the press to take a more incisive look at the presidential elections. Failure to do so might lead to the type of debasement that has crept into the other democratic institutions in the country.

The procedures for the election of the President (and vice-president) are well established. The Election Commission will set the ball rolling in a few weeks from now.

Press reports have confined themselves to factual narration of the composition of the electoral college and the weightage of votes between the elective bodies. Though deliberations of party leaders and pressure groups have been reported, attempts to enlarge the debate have been rather desultory.

This may turn out to be a costly mistake. Before the vote is cast (in a secret ballot) the public must make it clear to the elected representatives that further attempts at subversion of democracy by persons whom it no longer respects will not be tolerated.

The first, and possibly the most important, aspect relates to what is being referred to as consensus. The consensus of the early decades of Independence was altogether different from the consensus of today. The very connotation of the term has undergone a metamorphosis.

Too much emphasis on the need for unanimity in electing Presidents often goes against the grain of democracy. For, such consensus mostly meant imposition of the views of party supremos than a free expression of views.

With such 'imposed' consensus, the first citizen of the land becomes psychologically beholden to party caucuses. An element of *quid pro quo* does come in, more so if the incumbent desires a second term in office.

Since the worst fears of terminal degeneracy in the body politic have not proven to be unfounded, it is necessary to anticipate events in order to ensure that the office of the President is not dragged into sordid controversies.

Almost the entire process of governance at the political apex today seems to be concentrated upon devising stratagems to subvert the law and order apparatus of the state. In such circumstances, what sort of consensus should the public accept or the press champion?

There is still time for the press, and the public, to get more meaningfully involved in the presidential election. The matter must not rest in the hands of a few purveyors of power.

Every member of the electoral college must exercise his vote conscientiously. Under no circumstances must the office of the President become an object of unseemly controversy by the misconduct of the person elected to that office. The personality of the incumbent must not in itself become the cause for perpetual political strife.

Dignity and decorum must remain the hallmark of the person occupying the august office, which for a period of time in the near future might turn out to have more importance than the office of the prime minister.

Indian democracy is in a transitional phase. Only the deft hand of a universally respected person will guide democracy in the right direction in its reconstructive phase.

TERMINAL DECLINE IN GOVERNANCE MORALITY: THE APEX COURT AS UPHOLDER OF THE CONSTITUTION OR SILENT SPECTATOR!

This writer had been invited by the India International Centre to deliver a talk on "Reconciling Coalition Dharma, Good Governance and National Security" on 16th June 2009. Although the title was suggested by the writer, on second thought the title should have read, "Reconciling Coalition *adharma*..........". Hardly anybody concerned with the decline in governance would disagree with the statement that with each passing year the political leadership in the country as well as the quality of legislators suffers vertiginous decline, be it at the Centre or the States. The ills besetting political parties that in many cases have become personal fiefdoms are so evident that they do not require elaboration. What does need to be highlighted is that there is increasing lack of morality, or concern for the nation. Personal or petty interests sometimes disguised as party interests have become the order of the day. Several examples can be cited to substantiate what has been stated. The fact is that unless strong action is taken by practically the last repository of people's faith, i.e. the apex court, the decline in governance could reach a point where the unity, sanctity and security of the nation are overwhelmingly compromised.

The fractured mandate in the recent elections could give a fillip to indifferent governance, corruption and possibly even to selling the country's interest to extraterritorial entities. This is already the case in many countries in and around the subcontinent, elsewhere as well. Circumstantially, it can be shown with fairly high degree of probability that foreign interests could be dictating political decisions at the highest levels. This perception in the public mind is not limited to any one party, although some coterie based parties are likely to be more affected than parties that have a broader participatory and decision making base. The danger to India's national interest has multiplied in recent years due to the fact that enormous sums, possibly an order of magnitude higher than what was suspected earlier, have been siphoned out of the country and put out of reach of Indian authorities in safe overseas banking havens. What is more disturbing, however, is the fact that the very agencies required to safeguard national interest and bring the culprits to book have been subverted to such an extent that hardly anybody believes them to be principled or dedicated bodies working to safeguard the national interest. They no longer seem to discharge their duties impartially and honestly.

The state of affairs described above, which would be considered shocking by any reckoning could soon reach such proportions that setting the matter right might become a Herculean task requiring several years, perhaps decades, of upright people taking charge to reverse the decline. It would not have gone unnoticed that the leader of a major political party recently announced that his party would be willing to join any coalition that would dismiss the BSP government in Uttar Pradesh - that demand being the 'sole' criterion for affiliation. The brazenness of the demand did not result in 'any' political party declaring the leader making the statement (that is constitution subverting in its import) to be an outcast. To the contrary, leaders of most political dispensations are still busy wooing the said leader for joining their coalition. The next logical step for the wreckers of the rule of law would be to bring false cases against political opponents, or even inducing agencies concerned to manufacture evidence. By now the public has come to the conclusion that pursuance of criminal cases against politicians is no longer a matter of law or jurisprudence but a personal decision at the behest of quarters that run political parties or coalitions. The way the cases have progressed to date - on and off at the whims and fancies of the political masters - shows utter disregard for the majesty of even the highest court, which the people feel is either a bystander or - perish the thought - silent abettor, for reasons people do not like to spell out for fear of contempt of court.

To any objective outsider reading the earlier paragraphs the situation would appear to be as bad as in any banana republic or the most abysmally governed countries in the world. Strange as it may seem, the narration so far still does not reflect the worst danger the country faces; mostly due to the apex court not having moved far more decisively to set matters right. The nadir of governance has now been reached, where the police are construed to be the private enforcers for many chief ministers. The public have no trust in the police. The courts are seen to be equally helpless, fitfully coming to the rescue in extreme cases. The more immediate danger to national security, however, is due to political interference in the agencies constituted to safeguard the country's safety and the rule of law. It stems from the blackmailing potential that inheres - and appears to have been exercised - from foreign lands. It has been suspected that many of the country's political leaders, high officials and business people who have vast sums stashed outside the country illegally are amenable to blackmail from those in the know.

'Those in the know' includes people inside the country by way of close associates who may have helped in the illegality as well as foreign governments who make it their business to keep a watch on leaders of erstwhile Third World countries who can be *manipulated* by the knowledge gained. To put it succinctly, what is not known to the CBI and the Revenue enforcement agencies - or is known and stashed with the coterie masters who appoint the heads of these organisations - is *known* to foreign governments. At critical junctures, these foreign manipulators use the knowledge to blackmail the concerned minister and even those at the apex of governance to take decisions that are palpably not in the national interest. There have been many cases in the past where the public was flabbergasted by the inexplicable decisions taken that in the perception of the public and most people in the know seemed to be strange, to say the least.

Honorable Chief Justice, please treat this letter as a plea on behalf of MRGG and concerned citizens of India for immediate action to ward off the threats to the country highlighted above. These threats are likely to multiply on account of the complete immorality that now defines the political mainstream, including at the highest levels of governance. Such is the extent of the decline that upright parliamentarians, and their numbers must still be significant, are unable to raise their voice to stem the rot. Immediate steps that the Honorable Court could set into motion before the situation gets completely cut of control are summarised below:

- A judicial body or omnibus SIT to be set up by the Supreme Court to monitor and progress all criminal cases against political figures, some of which have been languishing for years and even decades. These should not be withdrawn, or progress slowed at the behest of the government of the day without the permission of the Court.
- Directions to the High Courts for similar action at the state level.
- A fresh and final date, say 31st December 2009, to be given to the Centre and State governments for implementing the directions for police reforms already given by the apex court. Where obvious foot-dragging is taking place an independent body of experts to be nominated to progress and oversee implementation under direct supervision of the Supreme Court and the concerned High Courts.

- Foolproof, non-tamperable, non-dilutable directions to the Government of India to ensure impartial functioning of the CBI and allied agencies in the national interest. In all sensitive cases a progress report to be given to the Supreme Court every three months. Where confidentiality is required in the national interest the deposition can be made to the designated bench or judges in sealed covers or 'in camera' sittings.
- The Supreme Court or a designated body to monitor on a regular basis the government's actions to repatriate the moneys stashed abroad illegally by Indian nationals or - taken out of India by illegal means. Where the apex court feels that progress is being delayed due to the leaders at the apex themselves being involved in the cases, directly or peripherally, methodology should be evolved to ensure that the files relating to such cases are not shown, directly or indirectly, to the concerned political figures. By the same token, as in the cases of judges of courts of law, the ministers concerned should recuse themselves from the concerned ministries, in the national interest. The fact that they should have been kept miles away from such ministries, in the first instance, goes without saying. However the coalition dharma of the day invariably puts the neta's interest above the national interest, and the number of fawning functionaries willing to oblige the neta keep growing by the day.

Since coalitions are always working under threat of withdrawal of support, even by smaller coalition partners, mechanisms will have to be set in place by the apex court to safeguard the national interest. Such action would *not* constitute undue interference in the functioning of the executive and the legislature. They are the minimum expectations of the Indian public to prevent constitutional breakdown or undermining of national security due to the increase in the number of legislators, and even ministers, with criminal backgrounds.

A stage has now been reached that legislators, many of whom have been elected with ridiculously low vote percentages in the first-past-the-post system come to the helm to take decisions that clearly do not reflect the interests of the country. The public has no recourse but to appeal to the courts to bring in a semblance of accountability to the process of governance; more importantly, to see that national security is not compromised at the hands of people who have plumbed the depths of criminality and degeneracy and yet end up as ministers.

Hon'ble Mr. Justice K.G. Balakrishnan
Chief Justice

RITUAL OF ANTI-CORRUPTION RHETORIC

At the recently held Congress Party Conclave at Burari the Chairperson categorically stated that corruption would no longer be tolerated and, in fact, they would declare war on corruption by fast-tracking prosecution and more words to that effect. On page 6 of Business Standard dated 21 December 2010 the following item appeared. Quote:

"Depts sit on graft complaints, says CVC

The Central Vigilance Commission (CVC) has voiced concern over central government departments delaying investigations in over 1,500 graft complaints sent to them by the anti-corruption watchdog, some of these have been pending for over three years. The highest of 117 complaints were related to the Ministry of Railways". PTI

Unquote

The figure is so high that it makes any semblance of dispensation of justice leave alone fast-tracking a big farce.

The Government policies of delaying or withholding sanction for prosecution of bureaucrats and politicians by the investigative agencies makes a mockery of the Constitutional Right of Equality before the Law. This practice, besides negating the very concept of justice and equality is tantamount to kick-in-the-teeth for the people of India and a frontal assault on jurisprudence. It cannot be condoned or allowed to flourish in any civilized society, leave alone the highly vaunted democracy in India.

In the light of the foregoing may we be permitted to request Your Lordship to immediately put a stop to this nefarious practice which, in essence, subverts the Constitution on which Indian democracy is based. At this juncture the Indian exchequer is being publicly looted by the very leaders who took an oath to safeguard the

Constitution and by extra-constitutional authorities who now wield real power in India. It is imperative that the highest judiciary in the land act decisively to stem the rot at the apex of governance, which if it went unchecked could undermine the sanctity, unity and security of the Indian state.

ABUSE OF SPECIAL PRIVILEGES

It is with utter disbelief that people read in the newspapers that exempting the three Armed Forces Chiefs from security procedures at civil airports has been turned down by the Civil Aviation Ministry. The defence minister, Shri A.K. Antony told the Rajya Sabha that the Ministry of Civil Aviation and the Bureau of Civil Aviation Security have stated that according exemption to the service chiefs will lead to similar demands from other authorities. In a written reply in parliament the government had disclosed the full VVIP list, including the President, Vice President, Prime Minister, Chief Justice of the Supreme Court, Governors and Chiefs Minister who were exempt from such security checks. The list also includes the Lok Sabha Speaker, the leader of opposition, Cabinet Ministers, Supreme Court Judges, Cabinet Secretaries, ambassadors and other dignitaries equivalent to the above positions. Through a circular dated September 28, 2005, the BCAS included the name of Robert Vadra in the list. The issue came up before the Supreme Court through a Special Leave Petition. Though the Court is yet to decide the issue, it was not satisfied with the government's explanation that the exemption list was based on the Warrant of Precedence as well as other compelling factors.

When countries in and around the subcontinent are falling like ninepins to military dictatorships and other forms of autocratic regimes India has remained a bastion of democracy. The reason for it remaining so is not on account of the worthy politicians and bureaucrats who have pushed the country into the cesspool of corruption and intolerable governance and, at times, anti-national activities. India is held up as a worthy example of democracy primarily on account of the pillars of the Constitution that have largely functioned in an exemplary manner, the foremost among them being the Supreme Court of India, the Election Commission and the Indian Armed Forces. As opposed to most countries in the world, be they democracies or autocracies, India will *never* be allowed to go under on this count because of the highest traditions of the Indian Army. The Indian Army has *zero* probability of subverting the Constitution, whereas, many functional democracies of today might yet be threatened with military takeover some time in the future. What is more, while most of the national leaders, parliamentarians and bureaucrats are increasingly held in contempt, the Indian Army continues to enjoy great respect among the people of India as well as among the nations of the world. To subject the armed forces chiefs to frisking *in* India, a practice, which no other country in the world would dare to attempt, is a national shame.

When this disgraceful decision was taken there should have been a collective outcry from the parliamentarians and the leaders of the political parties. That it did not happen bespeaks volumes for the execrable lot– there are always honourable exceptions–that run this country.

While serving officers must attend to their duties and not join issue in public in all such matters in the interest of good order and military discipline, the ex-servicemen and the rest of the country must not submit to this abomination foisted upon the nation. At the very least, it should lead to the dismissal of all those who were a party to this indefensible decision. An apology at the highest levels of government would be in order for not setting aside the decision *suo motu*. Even the respected President and Vice President should have intervened to express their dismay. Today the criminal elements have cornered a quarter of the seats in the Lok Sabha and the state legislatures. All parties field candidates with known histories of heinous crimes. Once elected, many of these worthies end up as ministers, even chief ministers. The day is not far off when one or more of them sit in the highest offices in the land. To become a service chief requires *full forty years of unblemished, courageous and exemplary service.* Are the petty myrmidons who rule the land trying to bolster their pathetically diminished stature by bringing down the stature of the service chiefs?

No other country in the world would have allowed such a disgraceful decision to go through the portals of government. The people of India must hang down their head in shame.

JUDICIAL ACTIVISM IS NECESSARY

The paper entitled 'Taking the PIL Route' is enclosed for information. I had first started working on it in November 2002 and have resurrected it in view of the controversy that has arisen on the subject of Judicial Activism. I am sure that Your Lordship and other Honorable Justices would be applying their mind to this aspect before finalizing the guidelines. I am of the opinion that in the ultimate analysis considerable leeway must rest with the justices of the Supreme Court and High Courts to treat each case on its merit. Inflexibility in the guidelines issued by the Supreme Court might retard the process of improving governance in the country as vote bank politics, vested interests and criminalization of the polity increasingly take precedence over the national interest and the cause of good governance. Enactments that should have been undertaken by the central government and state legislatures decades ago are only now being addressed due to the push given by so-called judicial activism. Meanwhile, in spite of several Supreme Court rulings on the subject, a body blow seems to have been delivered to the functioning of the CBI as would be apparent to anyone looking dispassionately at recent happenings, both within the country and outside India.

SPARE A THOUGHT FOR THE SECURITY FORCES

The situation in Jammu & Kashmir has deteriorated considerably, the reasons for the impasse having been aired often enough. The nature of the crisis is political. For that matter the majority of the crises facing the country result generally from political miscalculation, meddling or infighting; absence of firm handling during the incipient stages of the crisis, corruption, faulty governance and a host of similar reasons. In sum, in the vast majority of cases, be it the Centre or the States, the blame can be laid squarely on the political leadership. The security forces come into play when the situation has gotten out of hand. They are there to pull the chestnuts out of the fire for the political managers. And yet, time in and time out, they are blamed for either not acting firmly or at the other extreme for using excessive force. No doubt there have been cases of excess from time to time. However, to routinely put the blame on the hard pressed security forces can only result in their demoralization. Prolonged demoralization can put the state itself in peril.

Therefore, the time may have come to sit back and dispassionately review the conditions under which the security forces operate. It is a given fact that in recent years casualties suffered by the security forces, killed as well as wounded, have been on the rise. The government ordering their deployment remains blissfully unaware of their trials or tribulations. Take the example of the CRPF personnel deployed in Srinagar. The men have to be on guard day and night without respite. They are away from their families and loved ones for months on end in extremely hostile environments. It is not the agitators, but the security forces that are hunkered down, besieged by hostile elements from all sides. They face vile abuses. In spite of daily provocations they are required to show restraint. In 99 percent of the cases they *do* show restraint. Their mental condition is inadequately understood. They can never let their guard down, whether on duty or attending to their normal chores. The initiative always being with the hostile elements they can be stabbed in the back whenever they stir out or they can be subjected to bullets or grenades from any direction, at any time. Within the security perimeter they have been subjected to mortar attacks. In sum these are conditions that would drive almost any security force in any country to despair. The Indian security forces, by and large, show restraint that is *exemplary*. The truth of the statement becomes apparent when comparison is made with what is happening in other countries of the world, especially the countries in the neighbourhood. India's security forces, mindful of the responsibility they shoulder, have become inured to taunts and jibes from hostile elements. They have taken with equanimity revilement by the press and, occasionally, the public when operating in disturbed areas. There have been numerous occasions where the government of the day – or political leaders – to save their own skin have suspended security forces officers (in the paramilitary or police) or ordered inquiries against them without justification, as a placatory measure.

What emerges from the description of the conditions under which security forces have been operating is the extreme physical and mental stress to which they are subjected. So far they have been able to take the stab in the back from elements inimical to the country. They have been able to withstand tremendous pressures of the type that have driven security forces of other countries round the bend. What the nation's security forces may not be able to withstand indefinitely is a stab in the back from their own political masters, who have become adept at pulling the rug from under their feet with increasing regularity, almost across the political spectrum. It hardly needs reiterating that the political masters have let the security forces down at critical junctures. Were a deeper analysis to be made it would be found that more casualties are suffered by security forces, especially the CRPF, due to political ineptitude and thoughtless deployment than due to action by insurgents. An elaboration might be in order.

All units of the security forces, be they army or paramilitary forces, require rotation, rest, re-fitment and training after every two years of operational deployment, failing which performance deteriorates rapidly. After each operating cycle of two years under extreme conditions (for example J & K), if a unit of the CRPF is redeployed without having gone through a fresh training cycle 'as a unit' under their own officers, responsible for their training and command, it is bound to suffer heavy casualties immediately on re-deployment. In India, not only are units not given adequate time for rest, re-fitment and training after every operational cycle, they are actually tossed around like leaves in the wind, some times in penny packets in totally new environments and pushed straight into operations without elementary reconnaissance, liaison and so many other essentials of this nature. Therefore, blame for the casualties suffered in ambushes, where entire platoons are wiped out, can be laid directly at the doorstep of the ministry, up to the highest level. The culpability, in all such cases, is that of the government that throws them around in a cavalier fashion and equally that of the top brass of the paramilitary forces who do not insist on adequate training, rest and re-fitment after each cycle. The nation has to awaken to the state of affairs that obtains with regard to the deployment of the security forces and the ruinous effect on their morale and training due to the factors listed above.

Human rights issues are taken up routinely by human rights commissions, national and international NGOs as well as the press and the public. It is high time that the government and all concerned pay heed to the human rights of the security forces.

SCOURGE OF CRIMINALS BECOMING LAW MAKERS

Over the years it would have been realized that the political parties, irrespective of their hue, have no desire whatsoever to amend the Representation of Peoples Act to exclude criminals from the legislatures. Not only have the political parties ignored the public clamour in this regard, they have gone on to increase the number of criminal elements to whom party tickets are given, 'winnability' being the sole criterion for selection of candidates. There would not be too many democracies in the world where nearly twenty percent of parliamentarians in the central parliament and much higher percentages in the state assemblies happen to be legislators with criminal backgrounds. Should one follow the graph of the rise of legislators with criminal backgrounds in the national and state legislative assemblies, it is only a matter of time before such elements go on to attain a figure of 40 or even 50 percent in the legislatures. At that stage, India, which has already become one of the most corrupt societies in the world, would truly have gone under, with no scope for remedial action, short of revolution. The higher judiciary that would have allowed the country to come to such a dreadful pass would have to share the blame. That the danger is now life-threatening for the Constitution and civilized functioning is no longer in doubt. What remains in doubt is the role of the judiciary. The public is already at its wits end in finding a way out of the dangerous drift. Will the judiciary at the highest level remain silent spectators and watch the body blow being delivered to good order and civilized existence, nay, to democracy itself.

There are many PILs before the courts on the subject of criminalization of politics. We, the concerned citizens of India, now appeal to your lordships to *suo motu* take cognisance of our pleas so that the situation does not totally get out of hand. We do not have a system of referendums under our Constitution, but hypothetically were a referendum to be held on this issue, there is little doubt that well over 90 percent of the people would pray for deliverance from this scourge. We, hereby, request Your Lordships to set up a constitution bench to *suo motu* take up this question for consideration and deliver a clear verdict in the form of a directive to the Election Commission to disallow criminals against whom charges have been filed under the most grave sections of the IPC from filing their nominations for elections after January 1, 2009 or a cut-off date to be decided by the Supreme Court.

It hardly needs reiteration that criminals becoming law makers is *ipso facto* a violation of the freedom of 'ordinary' citizens that is guaranteed under the Constitution, besides being a negation of the principle of natural justice. The word ordinary has been deliberately emphasised to indicate that there is a whole category of the citizenry that now rules the roost, subverts justice, and can be categorized as 'extraordinary'; a category which is apparently outside the remit of Indian laws.

AFFIRMATIVE ACTION OR AGGRANDIZEMENT

The furore resulting from the decision to reserve another 27 per cent seats in the IIMs, IITs, and Central Universities, taking the overall reserved seats to 50 per cent has been reflected in practically every leading daily in the country. Screaming headlines and equally strong editorial comments in the leading national dailies on 8th April 2006 tell their story of the government's proposed affirmative action carried to a ridiculous extreme. Coming straight to the point, the country's IIMs and IITs have reached a point where they are globally renowned for the quality of the students who leave their hallowed sanctums. Unbelievably these institutions have almost overtaken the Ivy League colleges in USA and elsewhere, if one goes by the entry level salaries being offered by the finest global firms to the best and brightest amongst them. What is more, and such is their reputation, that on Day 1 itself the placements are completed across the board. In almost all other countries and all other societies the goose that lays the golden egg would not be killed in the manner that the HRD ministry and the government have decided upon. By and large there is an across the board outrage at the government's decision. It is axiomatic that excellence cannot be mass-produced.

In the light of foregoing, in my capacity as convener MRGG (Movement for Restoration of Good Government) and former Director General Military Training (DGMT), I pray for a stay on implementation of the government decision in this regard, while the merits or otherwise of the case are further examined by a larger cross-section of society. There are several important constitutional aspects as well that have not been taken into consideration. The most important among these is the right to equality of the majority. Majority has several connotations. It could relate to the majority denomination or the majority of students who appear for examinations to these institutions. In the latter case, if the majority of students appearing for the examination are from certain strata of society or they and their parents form the majority in holding the belief that intake into these institutions should be on merit through a transparently fair procedure, then the government order would be tantamount to abridging the fundamental right to equality of the majority.

There is another important principle of fair play, common sense and good governance operating in this regard. While not many people have questioned the concept of affirmative action on the part of the government per se, there have to be natural limits to such actions. In the opinion of this writer that natural limit for reservation for all categories should in no case exceed 25 per cent so that the right to equality of the majority is not impaired. Even the concept of reductio ad absurdum comes in. In this particular case, the government seems to have taken a quantum leap by reserving another 27 per cent seats, taking the total to 50 per cent. Regardless of all else, good sense and natural justice demand that irrespective of constitutional authorization for the government's action (wherever it exists) there be limits to what governments can do and must not do. For example, should vote bank politics sway the government of the day to move in a way such that the institutions that have taken India to the front ranks of wealth generation through the IITs and IIMs be crippled further by adding another 25 percent to the reserved category, thus taking the total to 75 percent, would the highest judiciary in the land remain a silent spectator or would it be obliged to intervene suo motu in order to uphold natural justice.

LOOKING BACK – THE LEGACY FACTOR

In spite of millennial domination by rulers of non-Indian denominations that came to rule India from across the seas and from across the formidable Himalayan frontiers, India's ancient heritage remained largely intact. Similarly, despite large-scale conversions at the hands of its foreign occupiers the vast majority of Indians continue to adhere to the faith of their ancestors. The ancient Rishis of India in the mists of antiquity revealed to the world the nature of *Brahman Chaitanya* (Cosmic Consciousness) several millennia before the rise of the Abrahamic religions that spread across much of the world in the last two thousand years. Vedic inspired denominations had spread beyond Indian shores prior to that, mostly in the East. But, as distinct from the spread of Christianity and Islam, the sword had no part to play in the Eastward expansion of Vedic thought and Buddhism. Nor did the pacific expansion of Indic thought lead to bitter interdenominational strife in the regions where it spread. It is important to keep this subtle but important difference in mind when examining the influence that an economically resurgent India might wield as the world moves deeper into the 21st Century.

An aspect that needs revisiting is the manner in which India got its Independence in 1947, at the time when the 20th Century after having seen two world wars was nearing its mid-point. Historians in India have attributed the country's independence to Gandhi's *satyagraha*. While it may be soulfully satisfying in an age sickened by violence to believe that India marched to freedom on the Mahatma's philosophy of non-violence, the attribution strays considerably from reality. India got its freedom as a result of Britain's exhaustion after the two world wars and its replacement as a global power by the new superpowers, USA and Russia. There is no way that Britain could have held on to its Indian empire much longer. The British Indian armies had played a significant role in the allied victories in the two world wars. Post-1947, had the British delayed the granting of independence, the battle-tested troops of the Indian Army – the Army that had underpinned Britain's world dominion for well over a century - would have soon rebelled, forcing an ignominious retreat on the British. There had already been a rebellion in the Indian Navy and the trial of returned INA (Indian National Army) prisoners of Subhash Chandra Bose had rekindled the spirit of fervent nationalism. The tinder being dry the call for an armed insurrection by a national leader would have led to a number of mutinies across the length and breadth of India. Had law and order broken down it would have engulfed the British. The two-century edifice of the British Raj would have crumbled overnight. It would have led to large-scale massacre of the British, something which was visited instead on the Hindu and Muslim communities when partition of India took place with the announcement of the Radcliffe Award in 1947. Because they left when they did the British went home in a blaze of glory with abundant goodwill for the Crown. They even saw their last Viceroy, Lord Louis Mountbatten appointed as the first governor-general of independent India. Such was the goodwill that obtained at the time of relinquishment of the colonial empire, that the leaders of free India went on to become the architects for the formation of the British Commonwealth of nations.

A brief introduction to modern India's birth pangs becomes necessary to understand the psyche of its leaders when evaluating India's projected rise to the status of a world power in the 21st century. To what extent would India's economic might lead to military might commensurate to its geographic size and population base? Will it emulate China's search toward hegemonic parity with USA, the unchallenged superpower of today? Are there limits to India's military power projection in the current century and beyond? If so who and what set those limits? These questions are addressed in the framework of the present global scene and its likely projection for the coming decades.

Although Gandhi continues to form an important part of the ongoing political and economic discourse taking place in the country it has to be said that in spite of the ideals of the Mahatma being quoted reverently at most forums where the future course of the country is debated, his economic and political philosophy has not found acceptance in so far as its practical application goes. Yet, at the end, it is difficult to think of an India that completely dissociates itself from the beliefs of the Mahatma, whether they relate to governance, sustainable development, harmony in pluralistic societies, or for the conduct of nations in the global arena. It is not surprising that Gandhi continues to attract the attention of so many people around the world, both as the man and the ideals that he stood for. Unfortunately, the debate around the Mahatma rages mainly around elements that were never put into practice in the land where they took birth.

Looking back on the events of the 20th century, both pre-and post-independence in India, one cannot fail in the impression that although he did not lose hope or his faith in his ideals Gandhi might have died a disillusioned man; if not disillusioned, certainly heartsick at the turn of events. Did the bloodletting that took place at the time of partition in the land where for decades he had preached ahimsa indicate that his philosophy had failed? It did not end with partition. The bloodletting continues to this day in every part of the subcontinent where the 'father of the nation' traveled.

India having veered so far away from the Gandhi's teachings it should have been possible to reject his philosophy out of hand and move on without a backward glance at an ideal that was considered impractical; or one that could not be put into effect in a land were shallowness, hypocrisy and untruthfulness have become the order of the day in public life. In which case, getting rid of the baggage of Gandhi's legacy and getting on with the governance of the country in the non-Gandhian pattern that prevails should have been easy.

This has not been the case. At the same time that untruthfulness and venality are in full cry, the very leaders who have propelled the country in that direction have not been able to dispense with the trumpeting of Gandhi's legacy because of a lurking fear that should it be discarded altogether India would not only have lost its way, it would have lost its soul. Then there would be no turning back. The thought of that final break, even shedding the pretence that is, troubles these peoples. They know that without the pretence they would not be able to face their countrymen, not at the hustings, not in public, possibly not even in private. At a deeper level they are not unaware that a final abandonment of Gandhi would be tantamount to condemning themselves to a karmic descent too horrid to contemplate. For, no matter how immoral the lot that governs the nation, in their heart of hearts they are deeply religious, albeit in a very warped sense of what their understanding of being religious should be. They also know that in India the vast majority of their countrymen revere the Mahatma and in spite of their poverty, deprivation and misery still closely adhere to the thoughts and ideals of Gandhi. For they are the ideals of Vivekananda, Sri Aurobindo and so many other sages and seers who moulded the character and destiny of India through the ages. The destiny that awaited India at midnight of 15th August 1947 has still eluded the country. Beneath the despair and turmoil that afflicts the land that destiny still awaits India. India many hope might yet produce the leaders who would take the country to the pinnacle that the Mahatma and the sages before him dreamed of in their quest for global harmony. The ideal, therefore, cannot be lost sight of. The ideals of Mahatma Gandhi are far too important for the redemption of India, if it is to find its feet and its true destiny. For the very same reason they are important for the world as well.

Meanwhile a fundamental change has taken place in the makeup of the people of India and the world. Nearly sixty years after Gandhi's death, the capitalist model and the morality that goes with it have become the norm. Even countries most staunchly opposed to it earlier have embraced it whole-heartedly, notably Russia and China. Could people of those days when Gandhi was popularizing the *charkha* have anything in common with Deng Xiaopeng's famous exhortation to his countrymen that 'it is glorious to be rich'. If it were glorious to be rich there would be nothing left of Gandhi's philosophy. If not the masses, at least the political class and the elite of modern India have embraced Deng's dictum as fervently as the Chinese in Beijing, Shanghai and Guangdong ; in many cases as strongly as the Americans themselves. Whatever be the reason for this departure from socialism to capitalism, it is undeniable that going back to the economic idealism contained in Gandhi's writings would relegate India to an economic decline from which recovery would be difficult in the world of today. May be, when consumerism that is fast overtaking the globe makes life itself unsustainable on the planet, people across the world will start reappraising the economic philosophy of Gandhi. That is why the world is not going to forget Mahatma Gandhi in a hurry. If the world has to save itself from self-destruction Gandhi's non-violence must become the leitmotif of a globalised world, and a reformed UN structure that would make non-violence between states the norm for the 21st Century. The United Nations has adopted October 2, the birth anniversary of Mahatma Gandhi as World Harmony Day.

Dear Dr. Quraishi,

we have interacted earlier on several occasions. You will be demitting office this year, if i am not mistaken. Possibly, the UP elections are the last major election that you would be presiding over. What satisfaction would you be getting after leaving the Election Commission knowing in your heart that you held free and fair elections for enabling the *mahachors* and *maha apradhis* to increase their strength in parliament and the state legislatures after every election. The ADR summary for this phase of the UP elections (one of many) speaks for itself. Democracy is on its last legs for the upright people of this country.

I have made the following proposal before to you in person, let me repeat it. After the results of the present set of elections are declared the Election Commissioners should sit together to review the results. During the review please decide to take a bold but necessary step to prevent terminal degeneracy from setting in our representatives and governance itself. As you are aware three entities have the power to bring in the desired change. The parliament or the political stream by amending the Representation of People Act to debar srious criminals (details as to safeguards etc. against frivolous charges and so on have already been outlined by you at several fora). With the vast number of elected criminals now in parliament such an enactment is very unlikely. The Supreme Court in spite of various PILs has so far remained a bystander. That leaves the Election Commission. On several occasions it has been stated in lectures, discussions, conferences and in a meeting with you that under the Constitution the Election Commission has been mandated to hold 'free and fair' elections. Free and fair elections are simply not possible with such preponderance of hard core criminals in the fray. Their initimidatory, financial and muscle power being enormous the question of fair elections remains a chimera. You have the liberty to interpret the omnibus consitutional mandate to hold 'free and fair elections' to exclude certain category of criminals as decided by the collegium of the elction commissioners, especially after having waited decades and with any number of representations to the powers that be to take necessary steps to set matters right in this regard. One of the most respected civil servants, the former Cabinet Secretary Mr. B G Deshmukh when he chaired a seminar in IIC, New Delhi a few years ago, in his summing up agreed with the contention that *freely interpreted* the Election Commission has the mandate to exclude hard core criminals from standing for elections. A former CEC was present in that seminar along with several other constitutional experts including Dr. S C Kashyap.

In the light of the foregoing, as Convenor, MRGG and Trustee NNFI may i enjoin upon you to rise to the occasion to save Indian democracy by (collectively) announcing that with effect from January1, 2013 the Election Commission would debar the given category (to be spelled out) of criminals, in cases where cognisance had been taken by a court, from standing for elections till the person's case has been decided. A decision of this nature (more suitably worded after deliberations) will not only be a historic turning point for Indian democracy, it would electrify the nation and energise over 99 percent of the nation's law abiding citizens.

Should some political parties or a body of criminals hold contrary view to the EC collegium decision they would be welcome to go to the Supreme Court for redress. It is the general belief of most eminent and informed persons to whom i have spoken on the matter that the SC, in all likelihood, would not only endorse the Elections Commissioners' decision but would more likely add a few caveats of its own to give teeth to the decision against future efforts to tamper with it or dilute it.

Yours sincerely

Vinod Saighal

Convenor, Movement for Restoration of Good Government and Trustee NNFI (National Network for India)
New Delhi

February 18, 2012.

Highlights (Analysis of Criminal, Financial and other background details of candidates)

- Out of the 360 candidates analyzed for the 6th phase of Uttar Pradesh Assembly Elections, 128 candidates or 36 % declared criminal cases against them. In 2007 assembly elections for the whole of Uttar Pradesh, 27% candidates had declared criminal cases against themselves.
- Amongst major parties, every party has given tickets to candidates who have declared criminal cases. SP has 31 out of 68 (46%), BJP has 30 out of 67 (45%), BSP has 20 out of 68 (29%), INC has 16 out of 34 (47%), RLD has 11 out of 32 (34%), JD(U) has 10 out of 34 (29%), Peace Party has 9 out of 46 (20%), Quami Ekta Dal has 1 out of 3 (33%) candidates with pending criminal cases.
- Out of these 128 candidates with declared criminal cases, 52 have declared serious criminal cases like murder, attempt to murder, kidnapping, rape, robbery, extortion etc. SP has 15, BJP has 8, BSP has 7, INC has 5, RLD has 6, JD(U) has 4 and Peace Party has 7 such candidates.
- Among these 128 candidates of 6th Phase who have declared criminal cases against themselves, ManVeer Singh of JD (U), contesting from Jewar constituency) has declared maximum number of criminal cases. He has declared 31 criminal cases including 14 charges related to murder. He is followed by Pushpa Sharma (BSP, Mathura constituency) who has declared 19 criminal cases including 2 charges related to murder and 4

charges related to theft and Shri Bhagwan Sharma (SP, Debai constituency) has declared 13 criminal cases including 1 charge related to murder and 1 charge related to rape.

- Among other major parties, the following candidates have declared the highest number of serious criminal cases against them: (1) Bijendra Singh (of INC contesting from Atrauli) has declared (2) cases against himself including two charges related to illegal payments in connection with election. 2) Yogendra Upadhyaya (of BJP contesting from Agra South constituency) has declared three cases against himself including one charge related to murder.
- A total of 210 candidates out of 360 analyzed i.e. 58% were crorepatis. In 2007, there were 22% crorepati candidates.
- The candidates with maximum assets in 6th Phase is Najir Ahmed of INC from Agra South constituency with assets worth Rs. 141.39 Crores followed by Vinod Kumar of BSP from Debai with Rs. 45.19 Crores and Mahesh Kumar Sharma of BJP from Noida constituency with assets worth Rs. 37.45 crores.
- Six Candidates have declared assets of less than 1 lakh.
- A total of three candidates out of 360 analyzed declared assets less than Rs. 11000.
- A total of 21 (6%) candidates out of 360 analyzed declared liabilities of Rs. one crore or above.
- Among major parties, the average asset per candidate for BSP is 4.81 Crore, for INC is 8.73 Crore, for RLD is 4.02 crores, for SP is 3.78 Crore, for BJP is 3.62 Crore, for JD(U) is 75.01 Lacs, for Peace Party is 56.11 Lacs, for Bundelkhand Congress is 11.49 Lacs and for Quami Ekta Dal is 2.86 Lacs.
- 52% candidates (186 of 360 analyzed) were graduates and above.
- Out of 1103 candidates contesting for 6th phase of Uttar Pradesh Assembly Elections 2012, only 85 (8%) candidates were women.

INDEX

A

2 G Scam, 161

Abdul Kalam, Dr. APJ, 213, 225

ABM Treaty, 149

Administration, 64, 90, 107

Administrative

  Council, 98

  Reforms, 151

Advani, LK, Dy PM, 210, 220

Afghanistan, 110, 126, 129, 130, 132, 150

  And India, 131

  Civilians, 126

  Police Officers, 126

Africa, 13, 52

Afzal Guru, 122

Airlines/Shipping Lines, 132

Alleviation of Poverty, 96

American Pilots' Bombing, 123

Ancient Rishis of India, 248

Anna Hazare Movement, 17

Anti-Colonial Struggle, 62

Anti-Corruption Rhetoric, 235

Anti-Terror Laws, 119

A-PIL, 114

Armed Forces Chiefs, 237

Arms and Ammunitions, 130

Art of Vote Bank Politics, 157

Asia, 53

Assam Bandhs, 167

ASSOCHAM, 188, 226

B

Backward Class, 136

Badal, Prakash Singh, Punjab CM, 210

Bahubalis, 64, 68, 70

Bangladesh, 109

Bangladeshis Infiltrators, 122

Bhartiya Janta Party (BJP), 23, 107, 143, 169, 170

  And Congress, 169

  Chief Minister, 23

  Government, 108

Bihar, 87, 108

  Andhra Pradesh and Gujarat, 143

  Model of Governance, 80, 85, 107, 199

  Polls, 105

Black Money, 117, 159-166

  Trail, 165

Bofors Cases, 22

Born to

  Misrule, 22

  Ridc, 22

Bose, Subhash Chandra, 249

B-PIL, 114

Brahma Kumaris, 102
Brazil, 16
Bribing for Votes, 9
British
    Cemetery at Lucknow, 169
    Commonwealth of Nations, 249
    Raj, 249
BSP, 100
BSP Government in UP, 230
Buddhism, 45, 62, 248
Bush, George W, 140, 148

C

Canadian Forces, 124
Capitalism 16, 23
Capitalist Model, 48
Carbon Credits, 13
Caste-Based Politics, 33
Casteism, 154
Central
    Bureau of Investigation (CBI), 65, 148, 151, 152, 153, 162, 183, 231, 233
    Paramilitary Forces, 142
    Universities, 83
    Vigilance Commission (CVC), 117, 118
    Vigilance Commission, 148, 151, 152, 159, 160, 161, 162, 191, 235
Centre for Media Studies, 11
Chief Election Commissioner (CEC), 11, 117, 162, 222
China, 16, 52
    And India, 13
    Non-Democratic State, 121
    War Debacle, 1962, 29
China-Italy, 110
Chinese
    Excesses in Xinjiang and Tibet, 61
    Growth, 28
    In Beijing, Shanghai and Guangdong, 48
Christ, 41
Christian Colonisation, 61
Christianity and Islam, 248
Churchill, Winston, 122, 123
CIA, 124
CISF Personnel, 196
Citizen-Centric Government, 201
Civil
    Aviation, 19
    Services, 32
    Society, 11, 66, 120, 157, 165
Civilisation, 40
Climate Change, 13, 16
    Conference, 13
Coal Reserves, 16
Coalition (s), 96
    Dharma, 139, 229
    Governments, 106, 221
Colonial Era, 59
Commonwealth Games (CWG), 25-28, 177, 178
    Charter and Functions, 184-185
    Composition, 179-183
Communal Divide, 69
Comptroller and Auditor General (CAG), 117, 162
    Report, 26, 181

Confederation of Indian Industry (CII), 188, 226
Congress
And BJP, 146
Coalition, 107
Party, 44, 160, 174, 206, 207
Constitution of India, 60
Constitutional
Right of Equality, 235
Vision, 41
Coordination Committee, 27
Corrupt Ministers, 32
Corruption, 9, 17, 18, 24, 25, 65, 66, 93, 117, 139-157, 160, 162, 171, 181
Court on Public Interest Litigation, 152
C-PIL, 114, 115
Criminal
Cases, 25
Class, 67
Episodes, 20
Criminalisation, 10
Of Politics, 83, 113
Of Polity, 23, 143, 144, 154
Criminal-Politicians-Bureaucratic Nexus, 145
Criminals, 152, 165, 254
CRPF, 241, 243
Cultural Plurality, 60

D

Darwinism, 119
Decision Making, 153
Degeneration of Law and Order Machinery, 113
Delhi
Citizens Commission, Text, 177-191
High Court, 182, 191
Democratic Institutions, 19
Deng Xiaopeng's Extortion, 48
Department of North East Region (DONER0, 168
Depleted Uranium (DU), 123
Depressed Classes, 141
Directive Principles, 42
Displacement of Local Communities, 13
Draconian Laws, 120

E

East Bengal 61
Ecological Sustainability, 16
Economic
Development, 13
Policies, 134
Education and Health, 82
Educational Institutions, 156
Election Commission of India, 10, 11, 67, 70, 82, 101, 105, 109, 139, 140, 141, 143, 147, 183, 215, 217, 221, 226, 238, 253, 254
Elections in UP, 67
Elections, 2009, 139
Electoral
College, 101
Reforms, 98
System, 104
Electorate, 17, 66, 80, 140

Electronic
Media, 9
Voting Machines (EVM), 98
Encroachments, 203, 205
Enforcement
Agencies, 163, 166, 183
Directorate, 160
Equality Before Law, 70, 152

F

Fall of
Berlin Wall, 149
Kabul, 127
FATA of Pakistan, 110
FICCI, 188, 226
Flora and Fauna, 24, 69, 92
Fodder Scam in Bihar, 109
France, 121
Freedom Fighters, 124
Fundamental
Principles, 42
Rights, 42

G

Gandhi, Mahatma, 44-49, 55, 62, 250, 251
Death, 48, 252
Legacy, 46
Non-Violence, 252
Philosophy, 252
Satyagraha, 248
Writings, 48
Gandhi, Rajiv, 154
Gandhi, Sanjay, 109
Gandhi, Smt. Indira, 149
Gandhi, Sonia, 106, 110, 209
Gandhian
Non-Violence, 49
Philosophy, 46-48
Tradition, 45
Gandhism, 46-48
Ganga and Januma, 24, 69, 216
Pollution Level, 216
Gangsterism, 143
Gaza and West Bank, 133
General Elections, 83
Germany, 121
Ghettoisation of Political Elite, 198
Global
Economy, 16
Environmental Standards, 86
Terrorism, 110, 128
Threats, 69
Warming, 13, 16
Globalisation, 41, 57
Godhra Incident, 206
Good Governance, 9
And National Security, 139-157
Fundamentals of-, 70
Gorkha Agitation, 167
Governance, 64, 65, 67, 113, 199
Issue, 117
Morality, 229
Governing
Council, 32-36, 71
Machinery, 63
Gupta, Indrajit, ex-HM, 200, 209

H

Haves and Haves Not, 60
Hazare, Anna, 171-175
Henderson Brooks Commission Report, 29
High Courts, 114, 115
Higher Energy Consumption, 16
Hill Stations, 24
    Darjeelng, 24
    Gangtok, 24
    Kalimpong, 24
    Nainital, 24
    Shimla, 24
Hindu
    Right Wing Party, 106
    Voters, 195
Hinduism, 169
History Sheeters, 68
Hizbul Mujahideen in Jammu and Kashmir, 126
Horse Trading, 9
Human Rights, 121, 125
    Issues, 243
    Of Security Forces in India, 125
Humanitarian Conventions, 119
Hung Parliament, 96

I

Idea of India, 39-62
Ideas of-, 47
    Sri Aurobindo, 47
    Vivekananda, 47
IED, 129, 136
Iftekhar Muhammad Chudhury, Chief Justice of Pakistan, 160
Immigrants, 125
Impact of Technology, 51
In-Country Networking, 50
Independent Oversight Panel, 162
India
    A 'Failed State', 160
    International Centre (IIC), 10, 11, 63
India's
    Destiny, 42
    Freedom Struggle, 62, 77
    Geographic Boundary, 42
    Geo-Strategic Importance, 100
    Image Abroad, 50
    Literacy and Social Development, 85
    Natural Heritage, 69
    Population, 69
    Relations with the West, 110
    Security, 30, 111
    Wealth Production, 142
Indian
    Armed Forces, 238
    Army, 81, 120, 121, 238
    Rapes Attributed to-, 120
    Border, 110
    Economy, 170
    Expatriate Communities, 49, 50
    Habitat Centre, 188
    Independence in 1947, 41
    Law Enforcement Agencies, 165

National Army (INA), 249
Population, 139
Presidential Elections, 2007, 99
Voter, 93, 109, 147
Indo-Gangetic Plains, 81
Infrastructure
Coordination Committee, 27
Monitory Committee, 27
Insurgents or Terrorists, 120
Inter-Country Networking, 50
Internal and External Security, 22
International
Atomic Energy Agency (IAEA), 149
Physicians for Prevention of Nuclear War (IPPNW), 16
Security Assistance Force (ISAF), 129
Threat to India's Democracy, 63
Iran's Quest for Advanced Technologies, 150
Iraq and Afghanistan, 124
IT Revolution, 50
Italian and French Models, 33

J

Jan Lok Pal Debate, 171-175
Jasmine Revolution, 171
Jaswant Singh, Foreign Minister, 208
Jihad Factories, 127
Jihadi Type Terrorism, 133
Jihadis, 128, 129, 136
Jihadist Forces, 124
Judicial
Activism, 81, 240
Activists, 215
Reforms, 147
Judiciary, 9, 21, 65, 70, 81, 86, 109, 113-137, 163, 180, 217, 221, 222

K

Kanishka, Air India Plane, 124
Kapadia, Justice SH, 165
Karachi, Pakistani Port, 126
Karmic Descent, 47
Kashmir, 125
Khalistan Bombers, 124
Killings of
Muslims in Gujarat, 23
Sikhs in 1984, 23
Kofi Annan, 103

L

Land Mines, 136
Landmark Elections, 2009, 139
Latin America, 13, 52
Law and Order, 87, 96, 109, 206, 249
Forces, 32
Law Enforcement agencies, 66, 135
Leaders of Globalisation, 54
Legislation—Security Threats, 135
Legislative Measures, 151
Lines of Communication, 167, 168
Local Communities, 13

Lok
Pal Bill (LPB), 17, 171
Body, 17
Sabha Elections, 2009, 37, 66, 72, 140
Sabha, 83, 96, 143, 200, 238

M

Madrasas, 127
Mafias, 147, 161, 166
Maharashtra, 143
Mahatma's Philosophy of Non-Violence, 248 see under Gandhi also
Mahavira, 45, 62
Malgovernance, 24
Manmohan Singh, 106, 107, 144, 145, 151, 207
Manmohan's Day, 144
Maoism, 146
Maoist in Red Belt, 136
Media in India, 121
Mesopotamia and Turkey, 122
Middle East, 54, 171
Ministry of Civil Aviation, 237
Minorities, 121
Minority Community, 64
Mitigation Technologies, 13
Moily Committee, 151
Money
And Muscle Power, 144
Laundering, 165
Lenders, 26
Monitoring Agencies, 12
Mount Abu, 101, 103
Mountbatten, Lord, 249
Movement for Restoration of Good Governance (MRGG), 9, 10 MRGG, 31-38, 70-73, 93, 98, 105, 152, 165, 179, 184, 185, 191, 196, 201, 207, 210, 212, 214, 232, 254
Aims, 32
Appeal to Indian Voters, 95
Appeal to Parliamentarian, 95
Questionnaire for Political Parties, 74
Criminalisation of Politics, 74
Down Sizing the Govt., 75
Electoral Reforms, 75
Environment, 74
National Security, 74
On Good Governance, 74
Population, 74
Transparency, 75
MPLADS, 154
Multi-Ethnic Culture, 60
Muslim
Clergy, 101
Invasions, 61
Muslim Voters, 195

N

Narasimha Rao Era, 154
National
Agenda, 71, 201
Emergencies, 67
Judicial Commission, 151
Network for India (NNFI), 12, 165

Networking NNFI, 179, 184, 185, 254
Parliamentarians, 95
Security, 64, 65, 91, 110, 111, 148, 153, 154, 159, 160, 165, 231
After 9/11, 174
Council (NSC), 72
Nationalism, 55
NATO
Countries, 111
Forces, 110, 111
Natural
Calamities, 134, 168
Resources, 13
Naxalism, 146
NDA Government, 151
Negative Vote, 214
Nehru, Pandit Jawahar Lal, 44, 55
New Master Plan, 210
Nigeria, 16
Night Vision Device (NVD), 221, 222
Non-Governmental Organisation (NGOs), 13, 114, 118, 155, 190, 191, 205, 225
North East, 167
NWFP (North West Frontier Provinces), 110

O

Operation
Bajrang, 126
Rhino, 126
Opportunism, 156

P

Pakistan, 61, 109, 125, 127, 155
And Bangladesh, 108
Army, 61
Pakistan's ISI, 124
Pakistani Actions, 125
Murder, 125
Rapes, 125
Terror, 125
PAN Identification, 68
Paramilitary Forces, 153
Parliamentary
Elections, 157
Form of Government, 41
Partition of India, 42
Pastoral Societies, 13
Patel, Mrs. Pratibha, 101, 102
Philosophy and Ideals of Mahatma Gandhi, 44
Planetary Destruction, 16
Pluralistic Society, 45
Poison Gas, 122
Against the Iraqis, 122
Police
Act, 1861, 20
Commission, 20
Reforms, 148, 162
Policy Guidelines, 35
Political
Bahubalis, 70, 225
Class, 67-70, 99, 154, 221
Divide, 67
Parties, 10, 11, 31, 50, 67, 88, 93, 94, 100, 143, 144, 146, 169
Philosophy, 44

Political-Criminal-Nexus, 78
Politics in Sports, 91
Polling Agencies, 34
Pollution Level, 69
Poor and Downtrodden, 93
Populism Vs Poverty, 108
Poverty Eradication, 75
Power Centres, 82
Preservation of Environment, 114
President Bush, 124 see under Bush also
President's Rule, 88
Principal Opposition Party, 100
Private Security Agencies, 124
Process of Revitalisation, 86
Public
  Interest Litigation (PIL), 9
    PILs, 17, 20, 113-117, 118, 142, 152, 163, 182, 191, 203
    Scrutiny Committee, 114-116
  Sector Undertakings, 18, 19, 83
  Services of Canada, 124
  Punjab
  And Haryana High Court, 19
  Assembly Elections, 210

Q

Quatrochi, 23
Quetta and Chaman, 1216

R

Radcliffe Award, 23, 249
Raina, Justice Rajiv Narain, 20
Rajya Sabha, 66, 83, 237
Recession, 16
Reforms, 151
Regional
  Disparities in North East, 167
  And Gandhism, 43
Religion in Modern India, 43
Religious
  Communities, 44
  Practices of Faiths, 54
Representation of People Act, 10, 145, 147
Reservations, 23
Reserve Bank of India (RBI), 23
Restoration of Good Governance, 114
Retaliatory US Exchange, 130
Revitalisation, 77
Rifle Regiment, 170
Right to
  Equality, 63, 65
  Information (RTI), 21, 189
  Information Route, 181
River System, 69
Role of Intelligentsia, 43
Rural
  India, 107, 108, 141
  Poverty, 107, 108
Russia, 52, 150
  And China, 48, 252

S

SAARC, 72
Sarkaria Commission, 86
Scams, 117, 165

Second Vohra Committee, 200
Security
  Agencies, 120
  Forces, 122, 241, 242
  Lapses, 22
  Of India, 22
Seshan, TN, Chief Election Commissioner, 118, 139, 140
Shadowy Organisations, 133
Sikkim, 167
Slum Lords and Mafias, 157
Smadhi of Mahatma, 46
Small Arms, 130
Social
  Justice, 60
  Upliftment, 114
Socialism to Capitalism, 48
Sonia Factor in Congress Victory, 106
South
  Africa, 16
  East and South East Asia, 13
Sreedharan, Delhi Metro Fame, 225
Sri Aurobindo, 251
Star War Technologies, 149
State
  Intelligence Forces, 146
  Security and Governance, 80
Sub-Casteism, 82
Suicide Missions, 131
Supreme Court (SC), 10, 11, 20, 29, 66, 67, 83, 110, 114, 117, 118, 122, 140, 148, 152, 154, 159, 161-163, 216, 222, 238, 243, 254
  And High Courts, 136
Sustainable Development, 45
Swiss
  Authorities, 159
  Banks, 26
  Lenders, 165

T

TADA, 92
Tagore, Rabindranath, 55
Tagore's Immortal Poem, 53
Tainted Leaders, 32
Taliban, 130, 131, 169
Tax Agencies, 65
Terminal Degeneration, 198
Terror
  Attacks, 22
  In Iraq, 123
Terrorism, 20, 64, 119, 121, 126, 135
  And Counter Terrorism, 133
Terrorist, 64
  Operations, 133
Third World Countries, 231
Third/Fourth Fronts, 139
Tibet, 121
  And Xinjiang, 121
Training
  And Good Leadership, 22
  Of Jihadis, 128
Transparency, 34, 151
  And Accountability, 171
Tunisia or Egypt, 162

U

UK, 103, 121
UN, 58
    Security Council, 59
    Structure, 49, 252
United
    Europe, 86
    Liberation Front of Assam (ULFA), 126
    Progressive Alliance (UPA), 25, 26, 99, 107, 161
        Government, 140, 152
        UPA-I, 151
        UPA-II, 151
        Coalition, 160
Unity in Diversity, 23
UP, 108, 143
    And Bihar, 68, 147
Uprising (First War of Independence), 1857, 169
US, 16, 49, 52, 54, 120, 121, 124, 125, 127, 128, 150
    Administration, 123
    And
        NATO Forces, 132
        Russia, 249
        Soviet Union, 149
        Western Forces, 131
    Clandestine Agencies, 125
    Excesses in Vietnam, 61
    Forces, 129-131
    Jihadi NATO Forces, 129
    Policies, 123
    Retaliation in Afghanistan, 133

V

Vajpayee, Atal Behari, ex-Indian PM, 106, 151
    Era, 106
Vienna Vote, 150
Vivekananda, (Swamy), 251
Vohra, NN, 199, 212
    Committee Report, 29
Vote Bank Policies, (VBP), 23, 154, 221
Voter
    Awareness, 9
    Intimidation, 143

W

Warfare, 124
Warlordism, 80
Welti, Philippe, 165
Western Democracies, 120
Women Empowerment, 75
Women's Emancipation, 96
World
    Harmony Day, 252
    Trade Cetnre, (WTC), 133
    War I, 122
    War II, 52, 58